ANCIENT BODIES, ANCIENT LIVES

Sex, Gender, and Archaeology

ANCIENT BODIES, ANCIENT LIVES
Sex, Gender, and Archaeology

Rosemary A. Joyce

With 35 illustrations

Thames & Hudson

Ancient Bodies, Ancient Lives © 2008 Rosemary A. Joyce

All Rights Reserved. No part of this publication may
be reproduced or transmitted in any form or by any
means, electronic or mechanical, including photocopy,
recording or any other information storage and retrieval
system, without prior permission in writing from the publisher.

First published in 2008 in hardback in the United States of America by
Thames & Hudson Inc., 500 Fifth Avenue, New York, New York 10110

thamesandhudsonusa.com

Library of Congress Catalog Card Number 2007905647

ISBN 978-0-500-05153-5

Printed in China by Midas Printing International Ltd.

CONTENTS

Introduction

About 30,000 years ago the people of Dolní Věstonice, a Paleolithic central European settlement (now in the Czech Republic), made the earliest known ceramics in the world. Ceramic figurines were found in profusion with the remains of mammoth-tusk shelters and hearths. Like all other Paleolithic groups, the people of Dolní Věstonice lived by collecting plants and hunting wild animals. The figurines they made included representations of women, also a common feature in other Paleolithic sites in Europe (fig. 1). Many such figurines exaggerated features of women's bodies: rounded hips, bellies and breasts are in fact the way archaeologists today identify these as images of women. From the perspective of a twenty-first century society looking back at an era when humans lived from the resources provided by nature, it might seem reasonable to assume that these people lived lives in which survival, finding food and reproducing themselves were of supreme importance.

Surely then, these amply proportioned figurines of women represented a society in which fertility (of the land, the game they hunted and of women) was supremely important. Perhaps women were valued (even worshipped?) for their ability to bear children. Perhaps this fertility even gave them high status and power. Such interpretations were once widely accepted. More recently, new evidence, the careful evaluation of old evidence, and a re-evaluation of the very questions archaeologists ask has enabled us to see these ancient peoples in a new light. It turns out that these were people skilled at making textiles, who likely valued such skills every bit as much as the ability to hunt or bear children. Instead of having possibilities entirely determined by their sex, perhaps the people of settlements like Dolní Věstonice lived varied lives in societies that

6

recognized individual abilities and accorded status on the basis of skills and merit. The work of many archaeologists around the world has begun to revolutionize our understanding of sex and gender relations in past societies like this one, and in the process has helped to question our own assumptions about "natural" divisions in society between men and women.

Stop briefly to consider what we might be able to say about the lives of men and women in ancient societies, where we have no written documents, from only the selection of things that were so durable that they lasted centuries, or even thousands of years. How, for example, can we know anything about textiles made by the people who settled at Dolní Věstonice, let alone know how men and women related to one another so long ago? The portion of humanity's past recorded in written documents – what we know as history – represents only a tiny fraction of the history and achievements of the human species, yet many of our assumptions about sex and gender are based on our own experience and the historical record. Archaeology enables us to understand sex and gender in ancient lives.

During their long, historically undocumented, existence humans may have had varied ideas about sex and gender. The work of archaeologists over the last two or three decades has done much to challenge contemporary assumptions that humans have always recognized a male/female dichotomy as the primary division of society, usually valued men over women, and understood sex itself in the same way. The task archaeologists set themselves is to interpret the scant remains of ancient societies and, by asking the right questions, to shed new light on the lives of men and women many hundreds or

1 Paleolithic European figurine, usually described as the "Venus of Willendorf."

thousands of years ago. Archaeologists begin by questioning whether we can make universal assumptions about the lives people lived in very different circumstances in the past.

Understanding the past without making universal assumptions

Hand-modeled fired clay figurines like those from Dolní Věstonice have formed a central part of arguments for a society in which women were dominant and religion centered on a mother goddess.[1] For those who advocate this explanation, figurines are depictions of an idealized, universal female body. The prominence of the female body as a subject is treated as evidence for the importance of fertility of humans and animals to the early hunter-gatherers who made and used these objects. Women's bodies, according to this explanation, are always seen as natural reservoirs of fertility, welcomed and celebrated in some societies, feared, denied, and controlled in others.

Assumptions like these focus the attention of interpreters on certain features of figurines – their fleshy bodies, rounded hips, protruding abdomens – while ignoring other observations, such as signs of age, indications of action, or details that result when different artisans create similar images. When we treat these objects solely as images, we also miss information that they have to offer as material products of the skill, knowledge, and labor of people in the past. The way particular figurine makers chose to suggest a human form, including details of the face or ignoring the face entirely, are as much traces of the work of individual artisans as they are evidence of the position in society of men or women who were their subjects. The choice of which features to observe and explain begins with the questions we think are open to debate, and which ones we assume are already answered.

Universal interpretations of figurines ignore the variety of different ways that images can resemble the things they stand for. European Paleolithic figurines appeal to us today because we immediately see them as portraits of human beings like us. In contrast, the earliest figurines from the Pecos River valley of the southwest United States do not resemble the human beings they represent in this literal, iconic, way. Instead, these flat, elongated ovals have only a few squeezed bits of clay to suggest facial features, with bodies covered by colorfully painted designs that today we can only suggest were specific symbols intelligible to the people who made and used these figurines. The Pecos River figurines referred to their subjects indirectly, through conventions not unlike the one that lets most people in the world today know that an octagonal red traffic sign means "stop." To interpret symbolic meanings like these, we need to have some understanding of the conventions that would have been shared by the ancient population that used such images. Even things that look like iconic representations can have symbolic meanings that are significant. Paintings in the European tradition that depict a mother and child have very different meaning when, through the addition of details like halos and lilies, the image can be identified as the Christian representation of Mary and Jesus as mother and child. Understanding past societies requires us to consider how ideas might have been represented in both literal and symbolic ways, and to recognize that symbolic conventions vary in different times and places.

The difficulties of treating ancient meanings as self-evident do not end with the intentions of artists. Different viewers may attend to different features of the same object, whether that is a figurine or the person or animal it represents. Some European Paleolithic images were originally identified as schematic figures of women with large breasts and featureless heads. More recent scholars turned these figurines over, showing that in this orientation they look like male genitalia – and, based on holes pierced to suspend them, this would have been the more common viewing angle when they were originally in use (fig. 2).

General models often project a modern preoccupation with differences between men and women on the past, ignoring the possibility that this binary division was less central at some times and in some places. Analyses like these can give an air of inevitability to one kind of sex/gender system. Paleolithic figurines immediately suggest identification as human images by resemblance, but ambiguities of

2 European Paleolithic object that can be viewed two ways. In this orientation, the viewer is led to see this as a female torso. Reversed, it resembles male genitalia.

viewing perspective, and even uncertainties about what was represented, are simplified when they are fitted into an existing model like the one that divides all human images into two categories, male and female. Even a figurine with abundant detail that allows us today to say "this is an image of a woman" might have been identified originally as an image of a specific person, living or dead, or as the personification of an abstract concept – like the representation of Liberty as a woman – or even as a representation of a category of people, such as elders or youths, unified by some feature we overlook today when we divide images by the sexual features that are so important in modern identity.

Putting things into place

At Dolní Věstonice between 28,000 and 22,000 BC, figurines were shaped and fired in kilns on the edge of a group of mammoth-tusk shelters. When detailed information like this is available about the place where things were found, the site of discard after the use-life of the object, archaeologists can create richer interpretations (fig. 3).[2] Fragmented figurines recovered together depicted animals and male and female human figures (fig. 4). Good explanations for these early representations should account for all of the imagery, not just some of it. We could continue to assert the "fertility" explanation that was proposed to account for Paleolithic female figurines by arguing that the fertility of animals was also important, and that the male figures are a complementary subordinate to the female figures. But the figurine assemblage can also raise different questions that suggest how much more vivid a picture of ancient lives can be when

3 Artist's reconstruction of a building at Dolní Věstonice, where figurines were made and discarded.

we take objects like these as evidence of the activities of the living, without assuming we already know what relations existed among men and women.

Analysts studying these figurines, the earliest ceramics known in the world, were able to reconstruct the processes used to shape and fire them.[3] Locally available soils containing clay were mixed with water and ground bone to form a very easily worked material. Inside a small building located at a distance from the rest of the settlement, this mixture was formed into small images, only a few inches long, mostly of animals such as lions, rhinoceroses, and mammoths (fig. 5). Small pellets of clay with fingerprints are the evidence of the maker tearing off sections of this material. A fingerprint visible on one female figurine falls in the size range for a child between seven and fifteen years of age, who touched it before the clay was dry. The shaped images were placed in a kiln, a domed hearth, at the center of this small building and heated rapidly to temperatures as high as 1500 degrees Fahrenheit (815°C). Because the clay was not left to dry completely, a large number of the figurines broke during firing, as the water trapped inside was converted into steam and expanded. The explosion of the figurine bodies is so common that researchers suggest that it was not a flaw, but a deliberate effect that the makers wanted to produce.

This research allows us to understand the firing of these figurines as a performance, during which many exploded, shifting our attention from their status as static images to their use in the lives of people. The skill required to produce figurines

4 A female figurine from Dolní Věstonice.

5 Fragment of figure depicting animal head from Dolní Věstonice.

would have been a potential source of distinction among people, a distinction we should not assume followed lines of sex difference. Considering figurines as material objects points to skill as a major source of distinction in this community. Other traces left in the same material add to this picture.

Fragments of fired and unfired clay recovered from the site were by-products of figurine production. They provide information about another technology: textile working. On fragments of clay, imprints of textiles used in the process of forming, drying, and firing the figurines were left (fig. 6).[4] With these clues in hand, archaeologist Olga Soffer re-examined figurines from this and contemporary sites and described in detail variations in the depiction of items of clothing on them. An entire technology that had otherwise vanished was reconstructed, the earliest evidence yet known for textile production.

Archaeologists argue that there were differences between women in these communities that were as important as any similarities among women. Artisans

6 Traces of a perishable textile imprinted on clay from Pavlov I site.

would have needed great skill to craft the complex textiles reconstructed. Other people might have been able to recognize the products of particular artisans. Not all figurines show representations of woven textiles. Archaeologists suggest that figurines with textile imagery recorded and celebrated certain women, perhaps those who actually made the textiles whose impressions were left in scraps of clay. Similarly, the skill to make ceramic figurines might have been a closely held body of knowledge of a ritual specialist, who reinforced his or her standing through the performance of firing exploding images.

These are far from the kind of universal explanations that assign a single meaning to Paleolithic figurines. In-depth research on ceramic and textile technology, based on clues that can be teased out from even the smallest fragments, leads archaeologists to consider *how* objects worked to create social differences without assuming that a specific kind of difference was primary throughout all of human history. Archaeologists do not even generalize the reconstructions of specific kinds of craft production at one site to all contemporary communities. The differences in skill that were required for the successful production of the figurines of Dolní Věstonice, and for weaving of the varied textiles in use there, cannot be taken as typical of communities across Paleolithic Europe without additional evidence. For archaeologists, differences from place to place sketch out a landscape filled with unique histories.[5] In those local histories, men's and women's lives could develop in many different ways.

Difference in practice

Paleolithic European figurines from different geographic locations depict textiles on different parts of the female body.[6] In eastern Europe, clothing on the stomach and breasts was common (fig. 7); in western Europe, the hips and thighs (fig. 8). Differences in figurines extend to whether there was evidence of clothing at all. Only some of the female figurines known (and none of the male figurines) have the distinctive features that record basketry hats, capes, belts, skirts, and bands tied around different parts of the body.

Archaeologists concerned with sex and gender in the past look as seriously at such differences as at similarities. One of the most significant contributions archaeologists make to the study of sex and gender is combating the assertion that humanity was destined to develop one way of relating men and women, a way that inevitably must be based on inequality between these two sexes and the domination of one over the other. They consider whether independent forms of

7 Paleolithic figurine from eastern Europe with textiles across chest.

8 Paleolithic figurine from western Europe wearing textile apron.

evidence give a single picture or suggest more complexity in past societies. They are particularly interested in contrasting representations of sex and gender with the actual practices of living people.

To understand better how the representation of human figures related to everyday practice in Paleolithic Europe, archaeologists compared the carefully documented differences of textile use on human figurines to evidence of clothing that would actually have been worn by people during their lives. These people had to wear warm clothing to live in glaciated Europe. Clues to the kind of clothing used have traditionally included fasteners such as buttons and toggles, made of carved bone or ivory, as well as tools such as bone awls (used to pierce holes in hides) and bone needles (used to fasten toggles to hide with some sort of fiber). The material evidence for clothing in burials contemporary with the figurines suggests that regardless of sex or age, individuals were buried wearing more extensive clothing than seen in figurines. This clothing is not obviously differentiated along lines of sex.[7]

We cannot just take the evidence of ancient figurines at face value: the real practices of the people who made them, and the way they chose to portray the people and animals they recorded in permanent form, were not the same. Difference between representation and practice is one of the clues used by archaeologists to improve interpretations of how images worked to create, reinforce, and even cover up aspects of social relations. Archaeologists studying Paleolithic Europe emphasize a distinction between human figurines with representations of textiles and those without such imagery as a first step in dividing the figurines into groups.[8] Female figurines are part of each of these groups, so by definition, not all the female figurines are the same. In fact, most female figurines, and all male figurines, lack any imagery of textiles. Archaeologists argue that this is evidence that particular women gained individual status from their skill at producing textiles, items of clothing to which they consequently had special access. This status need not have extended to all women as a category.

Visualizing difference

At Dolní Věstonice, not all animals, and not even all animals of economic importance, were subjects of representation. Archaeologists use the presence and frequency of bones from different animal species as clues to understand which animals these artists could have known, and which were the most important sources of food and other raw materials. Lions, rhinoceroses, and mammoths, the most common subjects of animal figurines, were selected for other reasons.[9] While the human images are recognizable as a few repeated kinds of people, many kinds of different animals caught the artists' attention. Diversity among animals was clearly more significant than variation among humans. Here, with a little distance from our own identification with human beings in the past, it is easier to see the selectivity of representation.

Rather than treating figurines as evidence of a uniform emphasis on biological fertility symbolized by female bodies, contemporary archaeologists present us with an image of Paleolithic communities full of people with different skills, that helped them stand out in their own communities. Some of these people were actively using visual media, like figurines, to represent variations among women, between women and men, between humans and non-human animals, and among animals.

Choosing to record some things, but not others, was a visual way to make some facts of life into topics of discussion. Figurines, from this perspective, were not just images of absolute givens, but ways real living people made claims about specific distinctions that may have been particular to a person and place. Visual culture was not a passive reflection of the way things were: it was a medium through which people shaped the lives they lived.

The distinction here is between two different ways of thinking about visual images. The first takes images as reflections of accepted truths. From this perspective, modern advertising images represent widely shared and accepted notions of the roles of men and women. But as this example suggests, we can instead (or simultaneously) think of images as a means for the circulation of propositions that might be contested. Not everyone accepts the kinds of ideals projected in contemporary advertising.

We might want to reserve this kind of active role for images for recent societies, where we recognize that there are many distinctions between groups within each society, and where we treat each person as having a unique perspective, life history, and identity, no matter how similar their circumstances might be to other people. But the same point applies to even smaller groups of people in societies with much less obvious internal differentiation. In the small indigenous societies in places like the Northwest Coast of the United States, most people are related to each other or at the very least know members of each others' families. Widely shared ways of depicting the animals that are emblems of different families make it easy even for outsiders to recognize raven, killer whale, beaver, and other characters. Yet the meanings of these images can be hotly contested between specific families or individuals. People recite different stories, sing different songs, and tell different histories about the same carvings, masks, and house decorations.

Contemporary archaeologists treat images as a means for the circulation of propositions that could have been contested, not simply as reflections of accepted ideas. We assume that assertions about human differences were open to diverse interpretations in the past, just as they are today. For contemporary students of gender relations, this is a critical basis for challenges to orthodox interpretations that might otherwise ignore complexities in human societies now as much as in the past.

Material histories of gender

The fasteners from long-vanished hide garments, bone awls and needles for sewing, and impressions of cordage and textiles, from Paleolithic Europe are clues to how people dressed in the long distant past. Such tools, by-products of production, and discarded finished products tell about more than simply the way clothing was manufactured. They tell us whether there were differences in the way people of different age, sex, or social status dressed. They are the traces left behind of the differences between skilled craft workers and those less adept. They can even point toward connections between the sites where they were found and others, more distant, where raw materials originated.

Archaeologists have developed ways to make objects speak, seizing on the methods other disciplines use to understand visual culture and texts and complementing them with attention to the making, use, breaking, and disposal of things. Archaeologists bring to the understanding of visual and textual documents expertise in understanding how humans shape things and things in turn shape humans. This book is about how archaeology addresses the needs of contemporary gender studies for an understanding of how people come to understand themselves as different from others; how people represent those differences; and how others react to such claims.

So Paleolithic figurines are treated not simply as images of ideal or real people, animals, and their interactions. Archaeologists look at images like these (and, where they are available, texts) as another kind of material object shaped by skilled hands driven by the ideas of people who were interested in persuading others to accept their points of view. Archaeologists make unique contributions to gender studies that are important both for our ability to imagine other times, and to understand how the way things are today can come to seem natural and inevitable.

Why exploring gender in the past matters

The lives of contemporary human beings represent only a tiny fraction of the history of the human species. Feminist scholars have argued that the relatively narrow concepts of sexual identities and gender roles common in modern western societies are by no means the only gender relations known from past human societies.[10] The experiences of people in the contemporary world are actually a good deal more varied than those expected under the normative two-sex/two-gender model. Nor perhaps is the normative model as deeply rooted in society or nature as its apologists like to suggest. Making that case, however, is not always easy, as the way gender is experienced today is homogenized, made to seem a natural given, and projected back into a timeless past of men and women living life as demanded by genetic capacities and reproductive imperatives deemed to be universal. Archaeological discoveries have often been part of this kind of naturalization, with even the earliest hominid ancestors represented as organized in nuclear families in which females were tied to home base while males ranged widely and brought home resources required by their families.[11] The reality of the past is much less easily assimilated to a single model of human society.

There have been forms of human life that today have vanished completely. Once there were no farmers. Even after farming was first adopted, many people pursued alternatives for everyday subsistence, ways of life we today call hunting and gathering or foraging and collecting. While some people today rely on similar strategies, they are not fossils living outside of time. Contemporary foragers live among farmers and within a world society in which power and wealth are unequally distributed. The effects of those modern conditions cannot be ignored when we turn to look at the distant past, when all humans depended on wild plants and animals for subsistence.

It is not only in the variability of ways of economic life that the contemporary world fails as a model for the past. Forms of political organization that are now universal are even later developments than the farming way of life. In the con-temporary world, small numbers of people determine conditions of existence of the great majority, often at a cost of consuming a greater proportion of the resources of their societies. Social relations like these, that place people in hier-archies including those predicated on sex, are fundamental to modern economic and political orders. Why should we assume that they were the same in times and places where modern economic and political structures were not in force?

Even historically recorded societies that share much with their modern successors had other ways of life than those today presented as norms. Ancient Greek societies, from which modern democracies trace their development and to which contemporary science and medicine trace their roots, understood men and women as different forms of a single sex, men developing that one sex differently due to a greater level of heat. Women were more similar to young men than younger and older men were to each other, since young men were still developing their adult sex. Sexual relations were accepted between adult men and either women or younger men based on this understanding of sex as a single potential developed to different degrees. At least some of the practices noted by historians in which women were disadvantaged socially, not able to own property, needing male guardians, and kept protected inside house compounds, were also inspired by a view of sex that saw women as inherently underdeveloped in contrast to men. At the same time, this view of people as realizing the same potential to different degrees allowed for recognition of variation among women. Enslaved women, servants, and women involved in the sex trade did not live the secluded, passive, and powerless lives of the upper-class stereotype. The Classical Greek concept of human sexual difference as a thing of degree, not kind, also allowed them to imagine a society in which women ruled and were warriors, the Amazons of Greek art and literature.

The contemporary world is the product of the past, not just a repetition of it. Modern economies, political organization, and social relations are outcomes of changing histories. We have no justification for assuming that life under the very different circumstances of even the recent human past was nothing more than a version of the world of today. Evidence gathered by historians and archaeologists about life in past societies provides many examples of different gender relations than the two-sex/two-gender model dominant in popular imagination today. Archaeology, with its ability to illuminate the entire history of the human species, is consequently a particularly powerful partner in the study of human experience of sex.

Archaeology and gender studies

When we think about the material past, what we have left today seems so meager: only the bones of a few people survive the centuries; buildings are represented by nothing more than ruins; of all the clothing, tools, and furnishings from previous generations, archaeologists generally recover only a fraction, broken, discarded, and seemingly no longer filled with meaning. This book is an exploration of how we might transform our thinking about sex and gender by drawing on the existing body of scholarly work about past societies that comes from archaeology. There are two reasons for exploring how archaeologists turn broken bits into clues to understand complex past worlds.

First, while documentary historians have produced rich accounts challenging common assumptions that the gender systems of today are universal, it is still true that documentary history can exploit only a tiny proportion of the history of humans on earth. Our species is understood to have achieved a distinct form hundreds of thousands of years ago; the oldest written documents we possess are from somewhere around six thousand years before the present. What happened before that time can be addressed only through archaeology. This includes the entire history of development of the potential for expression of ideas in visual and verbal form that distinguishes us from our closest animal relatives; the first steps toward cultivation of plants and animals; and the earliest experimentation with new forms of social life in which groups of people larger than parents, offspring, and their immediate relations lived in proximity in villages and towns.

Not all human societies of the past six millennia used writing to create textual records, nor were all lives documented in writing in those societies where literacy was functioning. The limited production of texts means that written narratives may be unavailable for much of human history, and for most people even in literate societies. Most of the human story is a story not recorded in words. Instead, the history of most human beings must be traced through the things they made, used, passed on to others, and discarded.

Archaeologists interested in subjects absent from written documents have developed skills that allow them to turn observations of things into stories about people. Nor is this simply a second-best approach to fill in the gaps where historical texts are lacking. Archaeologists have come to realize that the things people make in turn shape the people who use them. Much of the way we learn how to be men and women in any society comes, not through explicit discussion, but through the inexplicit experience of living in a world of things.

Insights from archaeology about the way materiality works on people can transform even our understanding of societies where textual history is possible. They allow us to see contradictions between stated norms and actual practices. They provide the context within which texts, themselves material things, were written, conveyed to others, read, and interpreted. The interactions that archaeologists can illustrate between material things and speech captured in written documents throw new light not only on the largely unknown past of human gender relations, but the present as well.

Modern concepts of sexual identities and gender roles have histories, and today's gender arrangements and categories are not the only way things could be or the way they have always been. Scholars from many disciplines have demonstrated that modern ways of being male and female were far from inevitable or natural. From Marija Gimbutas' proposal that ancient Europe was once a peaceful matriarchy, to Michel Foucault's genealogies connecting contemporary western sexuality to the cultivation of the male citizen's body in ancient Greece, to Thomas Laqueur's history of the relatively recent development of a model of two biological sexes in European medical thought, the past has been a fruitful terrain for arguments about gender.[12] Archaeology is one source of examples used in teaching about such alternative histories of sex and gender. But archaeologists have rarely been at the forefront in presenting these cases for audiences in women's studies, gender and sexuality studies, history, and other disciplines.[13] Partly this can be attributed to the fact that archaeology itself was relatively slow to take on questions of gender and sexuality. To understand why, we need to take a brief look at the history of gender studies in archaeology.

Doing gender in archaeology

Archaeology is not really a single discipline.[14] In the United States, archaeology has since the late nineteenth century been a subfield within anthropology. In most of the rest of the world, archaeologists can be found working on historical study of specific regions, such as ancient Greece, Egypt, or Great Britain. Whether academically associated in departments of history, Classics, or regional studies, organized as faculties in archaeology, or forming part of departments of anthropology, archaeologists worldwide are connected by a shared body of techniques, and of philosophical understandings of how the material they recover can be interpreted as evidence. The questions that evidence is used to answer vary among individual archaeologists, may differ between archaeologists working in anthropological or historical disciplines, and change over time.[15]

Despite this diversity, archaeologists communicate with each other across disciplinary boundaries and national traditions. So there are some common threads that can be detected in the global development of archaeology since its inception as a formal way to gain knowledge about the past, usually dated to the first half of the nineteenth century. In nineteenth-century archaeology, systematization of groups of objects, not unlike the development of classification in the biological sciences, accompanied the growth of natural history museums. The things recovered by archaeologists were valued because they were representative of cultural groups. Research was aimed at establishing the distribution of these evidences of cultural groups across space and through time. During the late nineteenth century and the early twentieth century, techniques were developed to arrange groups of objects in historical sequences.

What went largely unquestioned was that the goal of archaeology was to document the material culture produced by uniform groups of people. Variation within these archaeological "cultures," including differences between people of different sexes, was not of much interest. History was the sequence of cultures in an area. Men and women in the past were assumed to have similar life histories to those of people in cultures that descended from the archaeological examples. So from the beginning, modern gender arrangements were projected back into the past, usually without even being reconsidered at all.

In twentieth-century archaeology, systematic time-space documentation provided the material for new questions aimed at explaining observed patterns. Gathered and organized in terms of groups, the existing data encouraged explanations in terms of group behavior, without discussion of differences within groups. The lack of explicit consideration of assumptions does not mean that twentieth-century archaeology was gender-neutral. Archaeologists working before the late twentieth century did not usually identify questions of sex and gender as research topics. Nonetheless, they routinely proposed models of past human society in which men and women were assumed to behave in particular ways. They continued to take for granted that there were normative patterns in every society, to which people conformed. The normative roles of men and women were projected either from assumed universal patterns, or from observations of societies with similar economies and forms of social organization made by cultural anthropologists or recorded in historical documents.

The nature of the groups being studied was explicitly redefined in the mid-twentieth century, by archaeologists like those who developed the "processual" archaeology of the 1960s and 1970s in the United States. Instead of pre-existing "peoples," these archaeologists, under the influence of ecological sciences, wanted to explain the adaptation of human populations to their environments. This redefinition of units of analysis, which transformed archaeology, did not require re-examining assumptions about gender. These persisted largely unquestioned throughout this period of otherwise extensive reconsideration of the philosophy of archaeology.[16]

Some of the archaeologists interested in new questions in the 1960s and 1970s did start to consider that there might be multiple kinds of groups at different "levels" of the human-environment system. Kent Flannery began discussing households, groups composed of adult men, adult women, and children living together and sharing the work needed for subsistence, in his studies of ancient Oaxaca, Mexico.[17] Flannery's vision of life in the earliest villages in Oaxaca included defining specific parts of the interior of houses as men's and women's work areas, based on the presence of hearths and broken tools he assumed were typically used by men or women. Outside the walls of the house, Flannery identified house yards with storage pits as a kind of domestic workspace, again with specific traces of tasks carried out by men and women.

Viewed as the lowest level of economic adaptation, households were defined as one kind of lower-level unit. Task-groups, understood as specialized, permanent or temporary associations of people addressing a shared goal, were another. New units of archaeological analysis continued to be defined on the basis of what was shared, with less concern about differences among the people that made them up or even between the members of units of the same kind, such as separate households. But the definition of these lower level groups eventually led to explicit consideration of differences among people of particular sexes in these smaller-scale social units. In discussions of task groups, the sex of participants was often specified, based on comparison to living or historic societies.[18] So some forms of hunting were interpreted as involving groups of males who actually killed the animals, and groups of females who then reduced the kill to useful meat and hides. Households were understood inherently as composed of men and women cooperating for mutual survival and biological reproduction over generations.[19]

Archaeologies of gender emerge

While these discussions acknowledged the existence of different sexes in the past, archaeologies of sex and gender really emerged as an explicit area of investigation in the 1980s.[20] A number of studies of different regional traditions of archaeology have demonstrated that there were many, largely independent, moves toward asking questions about sex and gender in archaeology around the world.[21] Many archaeologists asking questions about sex and gender at this time explicitly disclaimed feminist inspiration. But it is hard to imagine, given the timing, that these developments were unrelated to global women's movements of the 1960s and 1970s. The international women's movement opened up opportunities to ask new questions for even those investigators who wanted to distance themselves from "politics," a goal that many archaeologists of gender argue is impossible to attain.[22] Increases in participation by women in academic training in archaeology and greater participation in archaeological research careers were products of the new political landscape of the second half of the twentieth century that corrected previous patterns of discrimination in education and hiring. Questions of gender emerged as viable research topics in archaeology in the 1980s and 1990s, most often raised by women, often women who were still in the process of earning their doctoral degrees. An early study of conference papers on gender-related topics by archaeologist Cheryl Claassen showed that literally hundreds of different scholars were presenting papers almost simultaneously, and most of these women were still students.[23]

The question most of these women originally wanted to answer was, "Where are women in the past?" To address it, archaeologists of gender rapidly devised methods designed to associate specific material traces with one sex. Because they began without reconsidering the categories they used, most archaeologists entered into this phase of research having made the assumption that there were two genders in the past corresponding to two biological sexes. Most also assumed that the activities of these two sexes, at least in part, would have been segregated.

Archaeologists quickly recognized that these assumptions locked them into viewing the past as a version of the present, and began actively to try to either justify or critique their assumptions. A proliferation of approaches has since emerged that range from maintaining a focus on women's pasts, because mainstream accounts continue to leave women out or take them for granted, to questioning the stability of gender identity, to critiquing the role of material things in promoting specific gender relations as natural. Today, archaeologists exploring gender and sex are following trails that lead to stories as diverse as the ways that freed African-American women remade family life after Emancipation in the recent past, how young men and women learned their adult roles in early villages in Central America, and how grandmothers may have started innovations among early human ancestors in Africa.

As a result of this scholarly activity, we have more information about sex and gender from archaeology than could easily be summarized by any one person. Instead, this book aims to selectively present archaeological perspectives on key questions in the study of sex and gender in the past and to communicate the actual excitement of this research. The chapters that follow are organized around issues, not areas or time periods. Some of the examples have been discussed in women's studies and gender studies scholarship, but are here examined from an archaeological perspective. Other research expands the scope of archaeological studies of sex and gender to encompass masculinities, and to question the two-sex, two-gender model. The perspectives explored come from the field and laboratory scientists who are discovering, documenting, and producing interpretations of evidence for histories of gendered experience. To follow the interpretations offered by these researchers, we need to understand something of the way archaeologists go about their work.

1

Ways of knowing the past

As a group of students and local laborers working with me excavate the broken household goods thrown away in an abandoned storage pit in the yard of a house, part of a small village at Puerto Escondido in northern Honduras last occupied around AD 400, we find a fragment of a small ceramic ring (fig. 9). Beautifully made of fine clay, the thin walls of the ring were burnished to a low gloss before being fired a uniform brown color. Other, similar, fragments of brown and black fired-clay rings are particularly abundant here. We recognize them as ear spools, cylindrical ornaments placed in a pierced ear lobe.

9 Fired clay earspool fragments from Puerto Escondido, Honduras.

opposite *10* Playa de los Muertos style figurine showing ear spools in use.

26

This is a piece of material culture of a kind that formed part of people's lives from at least 1000 BC to after AD 1500. Pairs of unbroken ear spools have been recovered next to the head in burials around excavated houses from as early as 800 BC. Small clay figurines made in Honduras between 1000 BC and AD 100 (fig. 10), and others made from 500 to AD 1000 (fig. 11), show human beings with their ears pierced and cylindrical ornaments inserted. When the first Spanish invaders wrote accounts of this region in the sixteenth century, they described similar ear spools still in use. These visual and textual representations, combined with the direct material evidence, allow fragments like these to be used as pieces of evidence for the way that people in ancient societies lived.[1]

In neighboring regions, ear piercing was described in the sixteenth century as a part of rituals in the lives of children. Rituals like this were part of the ways that children learned their adult roles, roles that exemplified different gendered experiences. The everyday use of objects like these ear spools was a part of the processes through which people were led to live their lives in ways valued in their society. Through the repetition of actions in which things like this were used, historically and culturally specific ways of acting, including those that varied between people of different sexes and were similar among people of the same sex, became taken for granted, naturalized.

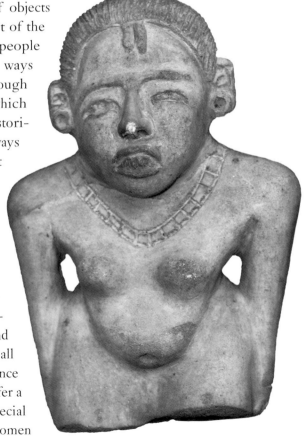

How do archaeologists move from things like pieces of broken pottery to understandings of the lives of men and women in the past? This small fragment of an item that once adorned a living person can offer a surprising glimpse of a special event in the lives of men, women

11 Late Classic mold-made figurine from the lower Ulúa valley, Honduras, showing ear spools in use.

and children some 1,500 years ago. The fragment of ear spool is, if you like, a clue, but by itself it does not reveal what we want to know about the past. Archaeologists look at the context in which an object such as this is found to reveal a surprising amount about past lives.

Archaeological context

Knowing that the fragments of ear spools described above were discarded in a house yard makes a major difference in their interpretation (fig. 12). While that interpretation should be related to the use of similar objects in burials at the same time, these particular objects were used during life and discarded. Without knowledge of their specific recovery site, we might be tempted to misinterpret them as "burial goods," a designation often applied to objects found with the bodies of the dead. Instead, we need to understand them as having had lives of their own, during which they were made, used, and discarded, and during which people's experiences and associations with them would have varied.

Researchers make the most of such fragile and fragmentary traces of ancient people's lives, using them as multiple lines of evidence.[2] The archaeological process begins with establishing a physical context for material remains. Whether locating sites in a region by walking through fields and examining exposed soil for things made by earlier inhabitants, or in excavating a site, the contemporary archaeologist is obliged to carefully document where material was when it was encountered. Things out of context lose much of their utility, which comes from their association with other things.

The household context in which these ear spools were found influences how they can be interpreted in many ways. As a residence, this was a place where people lived their everyday lives. "Household" is a categorical kind of context, allowing us to use commonalities between different houses to help fill in some of the uncertainties about any particular house. As a specific context, though, this household is distinct from any other, even if it looks very similar. These objects need to be understood in terms of their place in the lives of the people who occupied that singular house. So it would not be enough simply to say that ear spools were used in households. The occupants of any one household might be older or younger, richer or poorer, have more or less social influence or occupy distinct places in political governance. Differences of age, wealth, and status

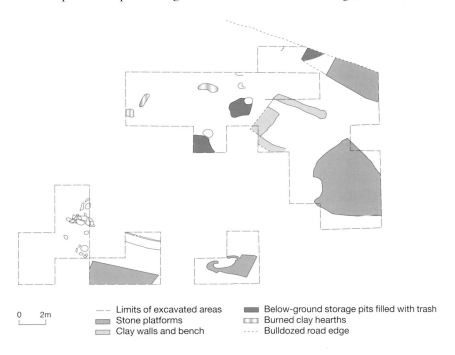

0   2m

— - Limits of excavated areas   ▨ Below-ground storage pits filled with trash
▨ Stone platforms   ▭ Burned clay hearths
▭ Clay walls and bench   ---- Bulldozed road edge

12 Traces of house walls, exterior hearths, and exterior pits filled with trash. Operation 2 at Puerto Escondido, Honduras.

among residents in the same house could have been as significant as any identity these people shared as members of the household. People of distinct ages, sexes, skill levels, and social relationships might have had very different positions within the household, and very different experiences in relation to objects like these ear spools and the situations in which they were used.

The context where we found their fragments suggests that these particular ear spools were disposed of after a special event. This interpretation can be made only because they were documented in association with the other materials discarded in the same pit. These included pieces of jars, bowls, and dishes, skill-fully decorated, expensive to finish and fire, used, broken and discarded at the same time. Bones of animals mixed in the pit contents showed that the meat of a wide range of animals was consumed as part of this event, including deer, the largest local animal hunted by these people.[3] The association of pottery vessels appropriate for serving food, animal bones, and ear spools in these pits suggests that this was the refuse of a festive meal served on a special occasion, accompanying a ceremony during which ear spools were used and discarded.

Context: Beyond place

The specific place where materials were deposited is only one part of the archaeological context. Every place in the world is connected to other places, and archaeologists can employ clues, such as the chemical composition of raw materials used to make tools, as a way to connect one locality with others. The wider geographic networks of the people living at a site at any single point in time are important parts of the spatial context.

Knowing *when* these particular ear spools were discarded is a further part of the context, and helps determine what other evidence from outside the local and wider spatial contexts is relevant. Based on the spatial and chronological contexts of things, archaeologists often use representations, whether in written texts or visual media, from the same time and place to create yet another kind of context for objects they want to interpret.

The regional chronological context places these particular ear spools in the middle of a long tradition of ear spool use that began by 1000 BC and continued for at least 2,500 years. Some figurines from both earlier and later time periods, carefully detailed in three dimensions, show cylindrical objects inserted through the ears like the ear spools found in our refuse pit. Other figurines, with less three-dimensional detail, just show a ring with a hollow center at the bottom of the ear. It is reasonable to identify these as more conventional ways to represent the same kind of ear spools, even though the view from directly in front does not allow us to see the long cylindrical shape.

Visual representations like these can illustrate how objects were used if conventions of representation, such as the elimination of three-dimensional modeling of the ear spool described above, can be understood and interpreted. Similarly, when texts are available, archaeologists can draw on descriptions of specific objects and actions to better understand material remains. But representations, whether texts or images, always were created for other reasons, and those other reasons may lead to only some of the uses of objects, and only some objects and actions, being represented. The fact of representation has to be critically examined to ensure that interpretations based on representations are not over-extended or taken as typical without independent evidence.

The ear spools found in the trash pit deposited in AD 400 at Puerto Escondido were certainly worn by some of the people who created the buildings, built fires in the hearths, and used the pots discarded in the trash pit. Figurines showing ear spools being worn had been made for hundreds of years at the site, from at least 1100 BC to around 200 BC. New figurines, using a different technology and different conventions of representation, would be made within 200 years of the creation of the trash pit, and these would again show people wearing ear spools. But in between, at the moment when the event that involved breaking and discarding ear spools around AD 400 took place, there is no evidence that figurines were being made, no visual images of people wearing ear spools.

This difference in time between the representations that help guide interpretation and the actual date when these specific ear spools were used needs to be kept in mind, as the way things were used can change over time. The continuity of ear-spool use even while representation of ear spools was discontinuous reminds us that representations are never simply records of what was happening, and raises questions we need to answer. The presence of visual representations of ear spools in use earlier and later at this location is a clue that at these other times, wearing ear spools was something subject to public recording and commentary. When ear spools were used and discarded around AD 400 at this site, there was no similar public visual dialogue. There could have been verbal discussions that have left no material trace. Alternatively, it could be that during the time when this event happened, ritual and everyday use of ear spools was more taken for granted, more naturalized, less a subject of commentary or debate.

Contextual associations raise questions that we might not otherwise have considered in trying to explain the contents of this trash pit. Contextual association of many different kinds of evidence has the power to expose questionable assumptions. So one of the core procedures in archaeology is the systematic pursuit of rich contextual information, including these kinds of spatial, chronological, and visual contexts.

Contexts of use

Exploration of the contexts of use of objects in the past, not simply the spatial context in which they were discarded or where they were found, is another way archaeologists strengthen their explanations. The reconstruction of past contexts of use is the most challenging part of an archaeologist's task. Archaeologists cannot rely solely on visual or textual representations to understand how objects were used. The clues needed are actually recorded in marks of wear and residues still clinging to the discarded objects, abandoned buildings, and even apparently featureless landscape where people lived and worked. These archaeological traces are the clues that can be interpreted as evidence of the use-life of things.[4]

In a featureless house yard, different levels of the chemical phosphate lurk awaiting measurement. They are the signs that human beings once worked in this space, leaving behind no other visible indication of their presence. Soil carefully collected from the same yard and examined under a microscope might show the presence of starch grains from corn, suggesting that one of the things done in the yard was the preparation of foods including corn. A similar microscopic examination of a chunk of soil, removed so that its layers stayed in place, could show signs of the bristles of brooms used to sweep away the debris that remained after the corn preparation was completed.

Archaeologists recover the objects they study at a stage in their life when they have been removed from continuing use. This may be because they were broken and discarded as trash, like the jars and bowls from the trash pit at Puerto Escondido. Or, it may be because they were taken out of everyday use while still intact, and placed in burials, tombs, or caches, examples of what archaeologists call structured deposits. Either way, the things archaeologists find contain clues to their use lives legible to an expert.

Broken pottery shows the internal color of the vessel wall. Gray or black bands show that the firing of the vessel was not continued long enough, or at a high enough temperature, for all the organic carbon in the vessel to be burned off. In the broken edges of the piece, small particles of sand or crushed rock, or more exotic materials such as tiny pieces of volcanic glass, are traces of the places where the clay may have been gathered, or the clay mixture prepared. Invisible to the naked eye, residues of liquids that once rested in the pot may still remain in porous clay, waiting to be identified as caffeine and theobromine, chemicals distinctive of chocolate drinks. Such material traces allow us to reconstruct an entire life history of the object from the gathering of clay and other raw materials, through the firing, use, and discard of the vessel. But reconstructing life histories of things is complicated, and different kinds of context are critical to making links between what we can know from these clues and the stories we want to tell about people.

Whether thrown away or deliberately placed in structured deposits, objects taken out of circulation do not always stay put, unaltered for the centuries or millennia that can elapse before they are recovered by archaeologists. Natural forces such as rain and wind or the action of burrowing animals may erode the soil from ancient sites, and redeposit it elsewhere. These or other natural processes may deposit more soil. Human beings may transform an area by digging into the soil, moving it elsewhere, or bringing soil in from elsewhere and burying an area.

These natural and cultural transformations of sites of human activity make the project of understanding what went on in the past more complex. Contemporary archaeology has developed a range of specialized methods that help to allow description of these depositional histories. These methods start with careful excavation by hand and detailed recording of the positions where things were located, in enough detail to allow the creation of reconstruction maps in two dimensions and models in three dimensions. Models and maps recorded precisely can be merged at multiple scales, giving archaeologists the ability to examine distributions of things across wide regions, individual settlements, and areas within settlements, in some cases down to the level of deposits that were the results of individual actions (fig. 13).

Uncovering the past

The people of Puerto Escondido in the fifth century AD were farmers living on the banks of a river that regularly renewed fields with sediment from the mountains far upstream. These villagers used some of the local clays to make a variety of things employed in their everyday life, even coating the walls of their pole-and-thatch houses with fine clays. The cutting tools that served them in the kitchen, garden,

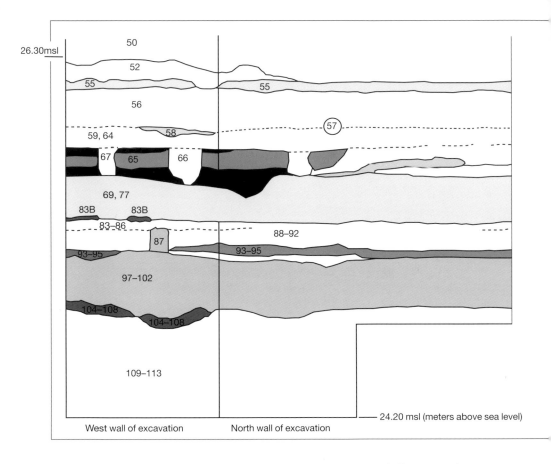

26.30msl

50
52
55   55
56
59, 64   58   57
67   65   66
69, 77
83B   83B
83–86   88–92
87   93–95
93–95
97–102
104–108
104–108
109–113

24.20 msl (meters above sea level)

West wall of excavation   North wall of excavation

and forest were made of stone imported from near-by and distant rock sources. Some of the objects they made in turn were sent to the houses of neighboring villages and more distant sites, where they had social connections. From time to time, they prepared festive meals and served them to visitors from near and far.

How do we know these things? Specific methods help archaeologists make connections between the local context of a site – whether that is a village, a neighborhood, a house, a pit, or a level within a pit – and broader spatial contexts. The objects that people used in the past were made from materials whose natural sources often vary slightly in chemical makeup. Sometimes the actual sources of raw materials can be identified, or at the very least, a region with similar materials can be outlined (fig. 14).[5] For example, stone tools found with the ear spools in the Honduran pit were made of obsidian, a black glass produced in volcanic eruptions. Minor differences in the chemistry of these natural glasses allow archaeologists to tell that material for cutting implements was entering the

History of deposits

50	Fill of Platform 4C-1, a plastered building, summit at 27.60 msl
52	Burned collapsed walls of Building 4A-1
55	Yellow clay eroded from walls of 4A-1, on surface at 26.10 msl
56	Fill below floor of Building 4A-1
58	Lenses of clay from Building 4A-3 on eroded ground surface
57	Eroded ground surface at 25.85 msl
59, 64	Fill below surface on which Building 4A-3 was built
66, 67	Pits dug through layers of refuse, from Building 4B? with decaying organic materials
65	Layers of organic-rich refuse
69, 77	Fill below these deposits
83B	Patches of clay from 4E-1 postholes
83	Ancient ground surface at 25.35 msl on which Building 4E-1 stood
84–86	Fill below this surface
87	Post hole, Building 4E-2 at 25.28 msl
88–92	Fill below surface on which Building 4E-2 stood
93–95	Lenses of refuse-laden clay on ancient surface at 25.15 msl
97–102	Soil deposited by river
104–108	Pits cut into ancient river bank
109–113	Ancient river levee

13 Sequence of deposits identified in Operation 4 at Puerto Escondido. msl = meters above sea level.

site from both near-by and far-distant sources (fig. 15).[6] Analysis of marble objects using similar methods gives complementary evidence of use of other materials from sources even closer to the site.[7]

The composition of the clay ear spools themselves could be examined using similar methods. Here, though, because ceramics are made of clays and other materials mixed during production, the distinctive profiles of chemical elements give a signature of a workshop, not a source for the raw materials. Such workshop signatures can be powerful evidence of exchange between different settlements, regions, or groups within a settlement.[8]

The potential of similar methods of assessing the chemical makeup of materials extends to understanding aspects of the individual lives of people in the past. Plants and animals have variable proportions of different versions of individual chemical elements, isotopes, in their bodies. These differences are due to variation in their environment and the way they process elements in the food, water, and air they ingest. When human beings eat plants and animals, they incorporate these elements into their own bodies. Trace differences in the abundances of elements in the original food sources remain, bound up in bone and teeth. Using one set of elements, archaeologists have long been able to suggest what proportion of a person's diet was derived from plant foods and what from animals, and to single out the use of fish and animals from the oceans from diets dependent on land animals and freshwater fish (fig. 16). Using a different set of elements, archaeologists more recently have begun to explore differences in where people grew up before they arrived at the sites were they ended their lives.[9]

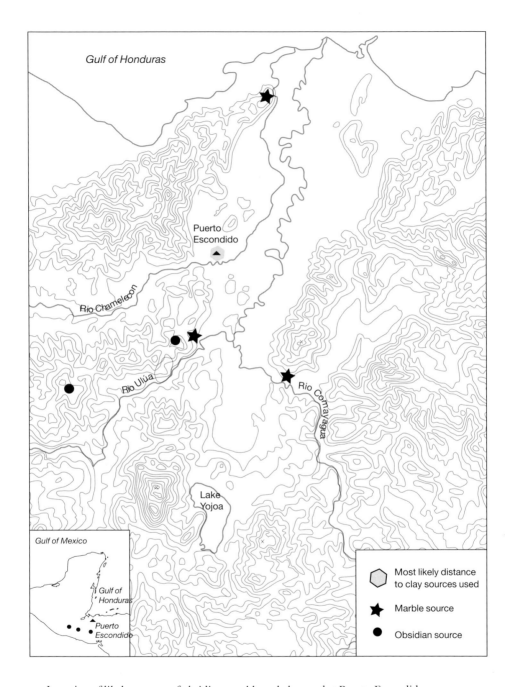

14 Location of likely sources of obsidian, marble and clay used at Puerto Escondido.

opposite top *15* Different sources of obsidian from Operation *5* at Puerto Escondido, determined by analyzing chemical composition.

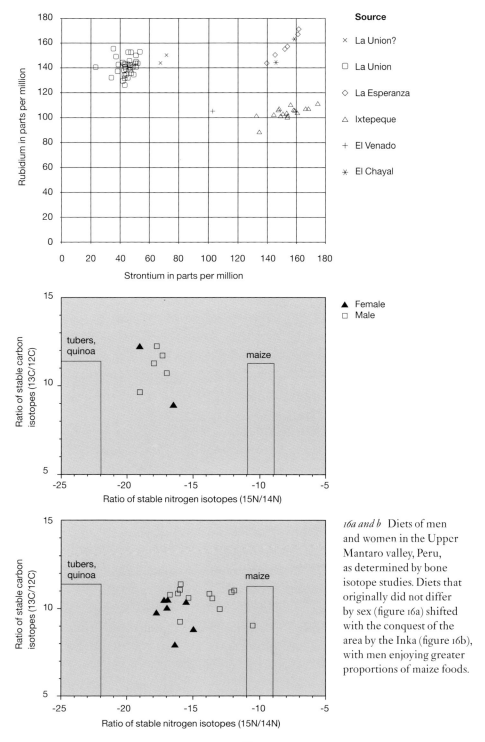

16a and b Diets of men and women in the Upper Mantaro valley, Peru, as determined by bone isotope studies. Diets that originally did not differ by sex (figure 16a) shifted with the conquest of the area by the Inka (figure 16b), with men enjoying greater proportions of maize foods.

Chemical analyses also provide archaeologists with the ability to see traces of materials used in particular areas, even when no other evidence remains except differences in levels of chemicals in the soil.[10] When people leave an area, they normally take with them all the still-usable objects they have. What stays in place most often, other than the remains of buildings, are by-products of activities people carried out. Processing food, sharpening tools, making pots, all produce microscopic residues that can be collected and identified by comparison to modern samples of such things as plant seeds, pollen, and even starch grains.[11] People often repeatedly carry out different activities in distinct locations. Because human activities may involve materials with distinctive chemical profiles, repeatedly working in specific areas can change the local soil chemistry. Even contact with resting human bodies deposits specific chemicals in the soil. The process is similar to intentionally applying fertilizer in gardens, another kind of human activity that can be detected archaeologically through measurement of different chemical elements in otherwise featureless soil (fig. 17).

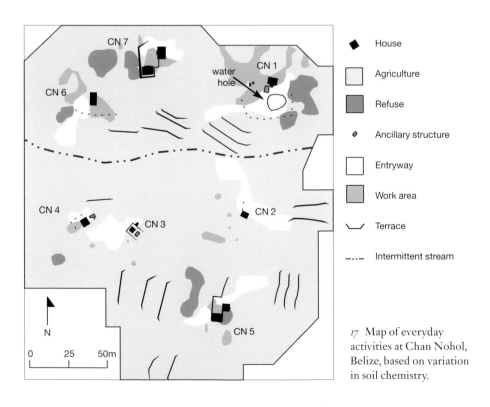

CN 7

CN 1

water hole

CN 6

CN 4

CN 3

CN 2

N

0   25   50m

CN 5

◆ House

▢ Agriculture

▪ Refuse

◈ Ancillary structure

▢ Entryway

▨ Work area

⌣ Terrace

–·– Intermittent stream

17 Map of everyday activities at Chan Nohol, Belize, based on variation in soil chemistry.

The strength of archaeological interpretations comes from the use of a number of such distinct lines of evidence that together provide a basis for ruling out some interpretations as unlikely, and that strengthen support for others. Archaeological interpretation at its best never claims perfect certainty; new information may change the picture. But archaeologists can demonstrate that some explanations are more likely than others, even when the humans whose lives they are explicating lived so long ago under such different conditions that we today have no immediate basis for comparison in our experience. It is this methodological basis that gives archaeologists the ability to talk about aspects of the lives of people in the past that may have shaped and been shaped by sexual difference.

Understanding sex and gender archaeologically

Classic Maya cities in Mexico, Guatemala, Belize, El Salvador, and Honduras had been abandoned for at least 500 years when the first texts written in European languages described Maya-speaking people in the sixteenth century. These early Spanish texts, and twentieth-century ethnographies of Maya people in the same area, describe a strong division of labor between men and women. Men worked the agricultural fields and, in more recent years, worked for pay on commercial plantations or other jobs. Women stayed in the home site, and processed the corn into daily meals using ground stone tools, hand-stones (*manos*) and grinding platforms (*metates*), pottery or metal griddles (*comales*), and jars. As well as these tasks, women in some communities spun thread and wove beautiful textiles. In a few communities, women made pottery vessels. Archaeologists interpreting archaeological sites have both benefited and suffered from the use of sources like these as guides in their interpretations of ancient gender relations.

For archaeologists interested in gender in the late twentieth century, particularly those whose goal was to identify women where they previously had been ignored, the task began with the identification of specific contexts where distinctive traces that could be attributed to people of a particular gender might be available.[12] For example, early household archaeologists used the distributions of tools used in food preparation (like the *manos* and *metates* of the Maya) as a way to suggest that certain parts of houses and yards were the spaces occupied by women. Such a search for an "archaeological signature" for women grew naturally out of the dominant approaches to archaeology in the 1960s and 1970s. Archaeology in those decades emphasized the creation of models as a first step before research was conducted. The preferred models would let archaeologists interpret observed patterns as evidence of particular processes. The use of such models remains a common part of archaeological investigations of gender, but as with other such "signatures," turns out to be extremely tricky. It is perhaps most useful as a beginning step that helps shed light on assumptions that are being made that should be reconsidered.

In the 1980s, the main source providing guidance for archaeological models was descriptions of men's and women's activities by cultural anthropologists. Using such ethnographic analogies is a fundamental part of archaeology, a mainstay for bringing material traces to life. But ethnographic analogies require consideration of problems in the sources of the analogy, as well as issues with the archaeological data to which they are compared.[13]

Analogy in theory

So-called "source-side" critiques need to take into account limitations of the ethnographers who produced the descriptions that provide the basis for interpretation of archaeological materials. These should include considering assumptions made when the ethnographers carried out their own research. One of the most obvious issues with ethnographic analogies for gender is the beginning assumption that every society divides people into two groups on the basis of a sexual dichotomy. This assumption was widely shared by anthropologists through the middle of the twentieth century. Ethnographers routinely described differences between people they recognized as male and those they recognized as female. Where the understanding of sex in a society was not dichotomous, the ethnographers' two categories may have contained people seen as different by members of the society itself. Where sex was not a major basis for grouping people together, differences observed between individual men and women, assumed to be based on their sex, could actually reflect other distinctions. Such things as age, social group, ethnicity, race, status, or skill could be more significant than sex for the identification of people with each other. In either scenario, the ethnographic source might provide a description of differences between men and women that, while accurate, was not rooted in differences between sexes.[14]

It was common for archaeologists to begin their studies, as their ethnographer colleagues had, by assuming that there would be differences between men and women in past societies. So these weaknesses in the sources of ethnographic analogy were not initially confronted. Archaeological use of ethnographic analogies suffered from further difficulties that had a disproportionate influence on models of sex and gender. The selection of a living society to use as a model has to be justified by some sort of correspondence between the ethnographic source and the archaeological target. Two main approaches to analogy, the specific and the general, developed and continue to be indispensable in archaeology. They also require serious critical examination.

When we understand a society in the past to be historically connected to an ethnographically described group, analogies may be made based on specific historical continuity. Of course, between the time that the archaeological group lived and the time that ethnographers observed their descendants, many things could have changed. These effects of history have to be acknowledged and if possible, disentangled from the model.

Analogy in practice

Historic and ethnographic descriptions dating from the sixteenth to the twentieth centuries were used as bases for models of women's roles in Classic Maya cities abandoned centuries before the first of these texts were written. What was not always considered were the possible effects of obvious changes, caused first by the reorganization of Late Classic Maya society into Postclassic society around AD 1000, next by the Spanish conquest beginning in the sixteenth century, and most recently, by the changes in these countries brought about by independence from Spain and incorporation in global economies. These historic developments created the new labor markets where men worked outside the home, meaning that models did not have a basis to accurately project men's actions in the past. Some of these changes may have involved significant reorganization of farming and even of the way food was prepared, a topic explored in depth by archaeologist Cynthia Robin. She demonstrates that the assumption that Maya men always worked the fields while Maya women stayed at home is most likely questionable. Examining historical changes also calls into question the exclusive practice of pottery production by Maya women. Most significant, ethnographic and historic European records were produced in political systems that assumed women did not and should not have political, economic, and social power, societies structured to attribute power only to men. The European observers writing historic and ethnographic accounts treated gender inequality as a given, and interpreted what they saw in terms of that assumption. In contrast, archaeologist Julia Hendon examined the clues that women accrued status at Classic Maya Copán through such things as the production of textiles. She showed that, when we consider that cloth was one of the main standards of value in these societies, unlike today, weaving was a way to create objects of wealth critical to crafting political alliances: cloth was used as gifts between ruling families and as tribute offered by subordinate lords to their superiors.[15]

When a direct historic connection between a past society and an ethnographic analogue is not believed to exist, general analogies may be made with groups that have similar ways of making a living, and similar degrees of social inequality. The emphasis on material conditions of life as the basis for general analogies stemmed from the understanding that materialist constraints forced societies into a relatively few ways of organizing social life if they were to survive. Archaeologists soon realized that the material world, while absolutely setting limits to survival, seldom forces societies to develop in precisely similar ways. There is substantial variability among people who are foragers or farmers. That variability precludes easily using one group as a simple model for another based solely on their similar economic situation.

Universal assumptions

Nonetheless, many initial approaches to an archaeology of gender began with assumptions about the division of labor between men and women that might be expected in societies with similar economies and degrees of social inequality. Starting with a two-sex model, distributions of tools and residues of production could be examined for evidence of division of tasks into two groups. Unless other evidence indicated a different conclusion, such two-fold divisions of work were assumed to reflect men's and women's distinctive tasks. This was considered especially likely if in societies observed ethnographically the tasks involved most commonly were the work of men and women.

So hunting was commonly assumed to be the work of men in early human history, and gathering the work of women. In Paleolithic European sites, this led archaeologists to identify cave art as the products of male artists because the subject matter – almost always animals – would have been of interest to the presumably male hunters. Women were assumed to have stayed close to the home base while all-male groups of hunters went out to bring back prey.

Women were considered most likely to cultivate plants in early agricultural societies (although they seldom were credited with domesticating plants), while men continued to provide meat from hunting and from the domestication of animals. Women were credited with making pottery vessels in early villages, while men were assumed to be the makers of stone tools. Traditional archaeological models tended to assume that as agriculture intensified, and production in some urban societies became more industrial, men would have replaced women. Men, these models proposed, would have controlled the products of labor and would have reaped any benefits, even from the work of women. Paralleling this set of assumptions about economic differentiation was a series of inferences about social life, all of which proposed that men increased their power and control as economies became more stratified.[16]

All of these implications flowed from observing dichotomies in archaeological distributions of material traces of different activities. In order to see women, archaeologists worked to see two kinds of tasks that were exclusively carried out by two kinds of people. As a consequence, archaeologists inadvertently projected into the past one kind of experience of gender, the two-sex/two-gender model most familiar to people in late twentieth-century industrial societies.[17]

A model of two sexes corresponding to two genders continues to be taken as natural even by some archaeologists, who argue that the dichotomy of sex is a fact that cannot be ignored. Biological studies actually suggest that we cannot simplify sex into a two-part division either among humans or among animals generally.

Understanding sex and gender biologically

Biologists estimate that somewhere between 1 in 1,500 and 1 in 2,000 births are of children with immediately obvious differences in genitalia from those conventionally expected for the male or female categories. The rate of surgery on children for whom doctors in the US decided alteration of genitalia was needed in order to fit one of the two conventional sex categories was 1 or 2 in 1,000 in 1998. Depending on what criteria are employed, the number of intersex infants could be even higher, with 1 in 100 diverging from the strictest normative expectations that all human beings should physically fall into two clearly marked categories.[18]

Anthropologists and archaeologists who became aware of contradictions between the two-sex/two-gender model and the ways people in other societies talked about sex differences tried throughout the 1970s and 1980s to arrive at definitions of sex, gender, and their relationship that would encompass all of the real diversity observable in human societies. These definitions often described sex as natural, biological differences between males and females, and gender as socially imposed understandings of biological differences. Different societies could, in this approach, have more than two genders, but genders were always constructions or interpretations of an underlying, real, dichotomy of sex. This tended to lead to the conclusion that gender was less real than sex, less consequential for people's lives.[19]

Sex, the term applied in these approaches to biological nature, was equally problematic. Originally intended to be the given, the natural facts that would stabilize social and cultural analyses, sex turns out to be much more complex. The folk model in Euro-American society, still shared by many archaeologists, holds that there are two sexes "required" for reproduction, and so people must be assigned to either the male or the female sex. That model works if one sex category is composed of people who donate an egg and the other of people who donate sperm, at least, as long as all forms of *in vitro* fertilization and surrogate pregnancy are set aside as unnatural. But the two-sex model ignores the existence of people whose reproductive organs do not allow assignment to either of these two categories. Claims of a natural biological dichotomy cannot simply set aside people who do not conform to a simpler two-sex model as "abnormal." Statistically rare bodies are still real, and describing some people as "normal" and others as "abnormal" is not biology, it is ideology. Even if we take the most conservative estimates as a beginning point, most human societies would have had large enough populations to include real biological variation that does not fit easily into two sex categories.

This reality is underlined when we switch criteria and look at other ways of defining sex. While reproductive anatomy is often the fundamental basis for asserting that there are two, and only two, dichotomous sexes, this claim is often reinforced by citation of chromosomal sex and sex hormones as also divided into two categories. The vast literature on variation in chromosomal sex in humans describes many cases in which individuals have chromosomal sex that is neither xx (normative female) nor xy (normative male), with frequencies again in the range of 1 in 1,000 to 1 in 2,000 for different alternatives such as xxy. These individuals may have three sex chromosomes, rather than two, leading to different patterns of development in some cases and being without evident effects in others. Even when a person has one of the two chromosome patterns that are treated as "normal" in the two-sex model, development may produce a body tha is unlike that of others with the same chromosome pattern, and more like the body of people with a different chromosome pattern. The physical development of individual people, including the development of body form, voice, and reproductive organs, does involve differences in the effects of sex hormones like estrogen and testosterone. But contrary to popular notions that there is a male hormone and a female hormone, every person produces the hormones that affect sexual anatomy and development. The production of hormones by a person changes over their lifespan, and may vary in response to environmental factors and behavior as simple as level of physical activity. Anatomy, chromosomes, and hormones do not form two simple packages.

Describing sex as biologically based may be absolutely true therefore, but totally unrelated to the claim that there are naturally two (or any other number of) sexes. Biological variability comes in complex and multiple forms. So how can we think about biological sex without creating some specific number of boxes and assigning everyone to one and only one box, for life?

A more realistic way to think about biology is to consider all of the variability we know exists as continuous, not discontinuous: ranges of variation, with each person standing at a specific point along a continuum. For every biological aspect of sex, not just reproductive anatomy, chromosomes, and hormones but also differences in body size or muscularity, we can imagine a different continuum, and we can imagine the same people resorted in different orders. All of these differences are real; some are categorical (like the xx, xy, and xxy categories of chromosomal sex) while others are continuous (like levels of different hormones or height). Some stay the same your whole life, while others change throughout life. Sex-based biological differences have material effects on people's lives. But they do not inevitably lead to any particular way of thinking about divisions of people into groups.

The fact that humans vary in these ways does not necessarily mean that variability will determine the ways in which people differentiate themselves from others. Experiences mediated by the body may be significant in one historical or social setting, and ignored or secondary to other experiences in another setting. We cannot start out with an assumption that people in the past placed the same emphases on certain biological experiences as people in the late twentieth century. The past becomes a much more interesting place to consider what sex/gender can be like in all its variability once we have realized this. In order to learn what the past can teach us, we have to challenge the effects that the two-sex/two-gender model has on our perception of evidence of people's lives in the past.

2

Goddesses, matriarchs, and manly-hearted women:

Troubling categorical approaches to gender

O n the southern edge of Mexico City in the 1940s, brick-workers excavating for raw materials at a place called Tlatilco began to uncover human burials that eventually were recognized as dating to the period of early village life (ca. 1100–700 BC).[1] Some of these burials included pottery vessels, figurines, and other objects. Mexican artist Miguel Covarrubias and other scholars saw the hand-modeled human figurines as indications of the lives and beliefs of the people who made them. Among the figurines were some with narrow waists, wide hips, and accentuated breasts, dubbed "pretty lady" figurines by some researchers and collectors (fig. 18). As with Paleolithic European figurines, they were treated as self-evident images of female fertility. While the social and economic conditions were quite different, fertility, according to many scholars, was just as important to people in early farming villages as it had been to early hunter-gatherers.[2] The fact that earlier hunter-gatherers in Mexico apparently never made figurines was not considered – why was fertility more of an issue for farmers in Mexico than it had been for their foraging ancestors?

During the initial period of discovery of Tlatilco, archaeologists salvaged data about over 200 burials excavated informally in response to what quickly became a huge demand from art collectors for the beautiful objects recovered. Mexican archaeologists rapidly took action, and conducted many seasons of careful excavation, lasting into the 1960s.[3] They added more than 200 burials to those previously documented, and were able to delineate precisely where these had been located within the local spatial context.

One question that the discovery of burials always raises is whether the area where they are found was exclusively used for burial (and thus can be identified as a cemetery) or if people were living in the area, and burying their dead close to home – a very common practice in ancient Mexican societies. Other traces of human occupation recorded by the archaeologists, including pits originally dug for storage in courtyards, suggested that Tlatilco's burials were originally placed in and around clusters of houses. Rather than a graveyard, as the original finds might have suggested, the contextual documentation showed that this area was an active village.

18 "Pretty lady" figurine typical of Tlatilco, Mexico.

The careful documentation of both the salvaged burials and later excavated examples allowed North American archaeologist Paul Tolstoy and his colleagues to demonstrate that the people whose graves were located had been buried over a period of several centuries. Tolstoy observed that there was a wide range of variation in the treatment of the dead, including in the nature and number of objects included in graves.[4] Most burials were unaccompanied by any objects. One or more pots were the most common contents of burials with objects. A much smaller number of burials had rare, imported, and carefully crafted objects, such as mirrors made of polished iron ore. Tolstoy, and Mexican scholars Mari Carmen Serra and Yoko Sugiura who followed up his analysis, showed that unusual objects, and the greatest number of objects, were found in more deeply buried graves, which would have required more effort to create.[5] Their conclusion was that already in this early farming village, there was a substantial degree of social inequality, allowing some people to command the labor of others, to collect rare, imported, finely crafted, and thus more valuable materials, and to take substantial amounts of possessions out of everyday circulation for use in burials. The burials with the most and the rarest materials were identified as likely those of people who occupied the highest positions in the society of the village.

As in all similar archaeological projects, these scholars used field and laboratory assignments of buried individuals to the categories of male and female to see how often men or women were included in high- and lower-status burials. Because this analysis preceded the conclusion of investigations by specialists in biological anthropology, identification as male or female was preliminary. In some cases, no biological assessment had been made, but objects in burials that were thought to be distinctive of men's and women's roles were used to assign them to one of the two categories. Tolstoy found patterns that suggested that women had high status in the village, and that they formed the core of the social group resident there. Men's burials were not as often part of the high status group, and he suggested that men might have married into the village. According to this analysis, Tlatilco was likely a matrilineal society, and women exercised authority in the village.

This interpretation makes Tlatilco a village where we have to think about the relationship between sex and status: if women had high status, as suggested by their burials, did they also monopolize social authority? While anthropologists avoid the words "patriarchy" and "matriarchy," this has not prevented others from interpreting villages like Tlatilco as evidence of the supremacy of women over men. As we shall see, though, the situation at Tlatilco is much more complex, and it is a good example of why it is unsafe to assume that sex was always the most important part of people's identities in the past.

Rethinking sex and gender at Tlatilco

Long after Tolstoy's pioneering work was completed, Mexican scholars published a complete catalogue of over 200 of the burials from Tlatilco that included assessments by biological anthropologists who studied the human remains. Interested in following up Tolstoy's study, I transformed this catalogue into a database and set to work to statistically examine patterns of association of features of the burials with sex.[6] The longer I worked, the more worried I became: nothing I tested ended up being securely correlated with variation between men and women. Only a weak association of some rare body ornaments – belts and ear spools (worn by a few males) and necklaces (more common in female burials than would be expected by chance) followed sex differences as determined by the biological studies. What had gone wrong?

Biological anthropologists and bioarchaeologists use relative size of adult skeletons, the thickness of features of the skull, and the apparent shape of the pelvis to assign burials to the categories of male or female, a procedure that necessarily has to set aside skeletal remains where these features are poorly preserved, missing, or otherwise ambiguous. This is also a procedure that can be used only on adults, since these differences develop over life, as effects of different levels of hormones that interact in development with other factors, such as nutrition and level of activity. So archaeologists conducting burial studies often rely as well on evidence from objects included with the person buried, looking for things they expect women to use and those they associate with men.

But there is a problem here. If we begin by looking for differences between men and women often we will find ways to discriminate between these two groups. But maybe the prior assumption that what matters is a binary distinction between men and women obscures other, more important, ways in which ancient people themselves distinguished difference. We have seen that even biological sex is not simply a binary: depending on what we use as criteria, we can define multiple chromosomal sexes, or place people on a continuum with respect to other indicators of sex.[7] So the question becomes, what groupings and distinctions were important at this place and time? The same statistical analysis that did not help me identify sex-specific patterns did reveal other ways in which the Tlatilco village was divided.

49

The people buried at Tlatilco included adults and children, some barely newborn. None of the children could be assigned to a sex category because the characteristics on which scientists rely develop at puberty. Not all of the adults could be unambiguously assigned to a sex category, either because preservation was poor, or the variability of the preserved characteristics was not distinctive enough. But even taking this into account, the differences in burials in terms of number and kind of objects included did not break into two categories according to sex. Having tested every characteristic I could for such a relationship, I changed my approach and explored all the variability in the information I had, to see whether there were *any* patterns that I could discern. What immediately emerged was distinction, not by sex, but by age. The highest number of objects and most unusual things were concentrated in the burials of young adults.

Why would this be? Like everyone else in these small villages, young adults were buried by those they left behind – their families. For those survivors, young adults were social bridges, linking families together. If they had lived, young adults – through the children they would have raised – would have united different families and created enduring kinship relations between them. Their deaths as youths left these social ties undeveloped, or just beginning. We can imagine the families that wanted to strengthen ties cooperating in funeral ceremonies meant to mark, not just how important these young people were, but how important the relations between groups through such young people were or would have been.

Older adults, regardless of sex, had fewer items included in their burials, and what was part of any one grave could be different from any other.[8] The most common shared features of burials of older men and women were clay rattle balls, recovered along the lower leg where they would have been worn while dancing. Other body ornaments found with older adults were more varied. One burial of a woman in her thirties included the lower jaw of an animal, pierced for suspension as an ornament. Bone beads formed part of a second burial of a woman in her thirties, along with clay rattles. A third woman, estimated to have died around age thirty-nine, wore shell beads, again not duplicated in any other burial, along with her clay rattles.

While these mature women shared some features of burial – including, in some cases, having pots or figurines in their graves – some of the oldest women were treated in truly unique ways. They were much more likely to be buried in isolated graves, away from the clusters of burials near or under house floors. One woman in her forties, quite old for this village, was buried along with two dogs. The skull of another older woman was reburied with a stone object used in playing the ritual ballgame, placed in an area away from the more common groups of burials of youths and young adults.

The same objects were used in burials of males and females of similar ages, like the rattle balls found with older men and women. Men and women both had objects that archaeologists expected to find only with men or only with women. Rather than a matriarchal society, Tlatilco seems better understood as a society in which sex was less significant than age as a basis for identification among people.

Gender identity and difference

Looking for women in Classic Maya society, archaeologists used portraits of royal or noble women, and tools for tasks such as spinning, weaving, and corn grinding as clues to women's presence and actions. Other archaeological studies questioned whether all the people included in a group defined as sharing a gender identity had more in common with each other than they did with members of the "other" sex. Classic Maya noblewomen did spin and weave, but their work produced cloth used in political ceremonies, not just the raw material for their family's clothing. Their social status as members of powerful families made their experiences as spinners and weavers potentially very different from that of women in farming households.[9]

We cannot begin our exploration of gender in archaeology by just looking for women and men, because that assumes that one kind of gender relations is universal, timeless, and more important than any other form of social distinction. How, then, can we make a start at investigating the lived experience of gender in the past? We might consider whether what we are trying to understand is gender identity or difference. An interest in gender identity makes us look for what men have in common, or what women have in common, taking those shared experiences as more important than differences among men or among women. An interest in how men's and women's experiences vary leads us in a very different direction. We have to be interested not only in how men differ from women, but how experiences vary among people whose bodily sex is similar, and who we might assign to a single biological category "male" or "female."

Models of gender identity emphasize commonalities, such as those among women, usually conceived of as one half of a dichotomy with men, that encompasses all people in an either/or fashion. Models of difference instead offer a framework in which other characteristics, such as age, race, and class, can be considered at the same time as gender. A person may have much in common with others whose physical sexual characteristics are distinct, as when the ancient Greeks grouped women and beardless youths together as potential sexual partners of more mature men. Simultaneously, people who share a position in regard to sex or gender may have great variation in other aspects of their social identity, for example, age differences between young men and adult women in ancient Greece.

Paleolithic figurines such as those from Dolní Věstonice, some of the earliest representations of human beings, have provided evidence for discussions of gender identity as well as difference. The image of the "Venus of Willendorf" is immediately recognizable to people far removed from academic archaeology (see fig. 1). With its exaggerated breasts, contemporary viewers understand it as clearly defining a female identity. Taken as an idealization of femininity, it has been easily assimilated to contemporary ideas about sex and gender, even to the point of being considered a form of early pornography.[10] This interpretation defines a single way of being female and this universalized female role places biological reproduction and generalized fertility at the core of a feminine identity shared by all women.[11] This single femininity is assumed to stand in relation to an alternative, opposite, singular way of being male.

Because they are viewed from the outset as being "about" the category "woman," Paleolithic figurines like these, and figurines from the Neolithic villages that developed after 10,000 BC in some areas of Europe, are also used as evidence that there once existed a matriarchal society in this area that has subsequently been disrupted.[12] "Matriarchy" here implies that women, revered for their inherent fertility, were the sole sources of authority. In this model, men and women shared a reverence for a Mother Goddess, sometimes considered to be the actual subject of representation in figurines (fig. 19). As developed in most detail by Marija Gimbutas, this interpretation of gender in the European past is an extreme example of a number of features common in archaeological work on gender.

In studies like these, human representations are taken as key evidence of social realities. Humans are separated from other subjects of representation, such as the animals represented at Dolní Věstonice, and given a distinct kind of explanation. Authors of these arguments assume that human representations are intended to communicate sexual identity because sexual identity is taken to be the most fundamental way human societies are divided. So the first question an archaeologist following such an approach has about figurines is, "what features mark the sex of the person shown?"

Why we find one sex when we look for two

Following a categorical model of dichotomous sex, the features singled out are usually secondary sexual characteristics: developed breasts and hips for females, the lack of these and presence of facial hair for males. The identification of figurines as female also depends on the absence of any features suggesting male sexual organs. These primary sexual characteristics complement the secondary features of facial hair as evidence for male identity in a relatively small number

19 Female figurine from Neolithic Çatal Hüyük, Turkey, often interpreted as a Mother Goddess.

of cases. More often, the absence of features suggesting developed breasts or hips is taken as confirming male sexual identity.

In interpretations like this, the assumption is that people in the past shared with the present a gender system that divides human beings into two opposing categories based on reproductive sexuality. Breasts, hips, and buttocks become sites for identifying female bodies; genitalia and facial hair serve as signs of maleness. The presence of any one of these is enough to allow assignment to one category or the other.

What this means is that we can never discover alternative concepts of gender, because we are always forcing the actual evidence to fit a pre-existing model. Under such a dichotomous model of two sexes, a mixture of features in a figurine would be unintelligible. Maleness is given special emphasis. Any male signifier outweighs any of the traits considered typical of females.

Maleness becomes the only really solid category. All the figurines lacking male traits are defined by that lack as female. So a figurine with an otherwise featureless body and schematic torso may automatically be identified as female (fig. 20). This leads to a predictable pattern of identifying much greater numbers of female figurines than of male figurines, since the latter require more specific features for identification. Figurines not assigned to one or another of the

20 Schematic figurines identified as female, from the Archaic Pecos River Culture, Texas.

dichotomous categories can only be characterized as "unidentifiable." We cannot even consider the possibility that they might form a different category or categories altogether, and we cannot even imagine other ways of thinking about identity and representing variation in it. Bioarchaeologists always at least have an undifferentiated juvenile category, and may actually divide human remains up based on the degree of certainty in assignment to male or female sex. In figurine studies, it would seem that more certainty about assignment to two sexes is possible than when we have the actual skeletal remains of living people. How could it be that sex – conceived of as a natural, biological fact – is messier in the flesh than it is in artistic representation?

In the interpretive model of an old European cult of the Mother Goddess, differences in the body forms of the figurines identified as female become the basis to define different stages in the life of the goddess or of women granted prestige as representations of the goddess. The absence of secondary sexual characteristics becomes the basis to identify a youthful, pre-reproductive life stage of the goddess. The production of figurines showing different life stages then serves to reinforce the importance of women's fertility in these societies. Girls and women are primarily understood as potentially or actively mothers.

Even though the intent is to argue for a higher prestige for women at this point in the past than in later periods, the outcome of this approach is to attribute timelessness to one modern form of gender relations. Variability among women is considered entirely in terms of reproduction and fertility, which may not have been the central experiences of every woman's life. The experiences of males are reconstructed solely as the complement to those of women. This interpretation does not even consider the possibility that at this moment in human history, social life might have been organized in such a way that sex was not the primary basis for identification between people. We are locked into considering one kind of experience as automatically shared by all women – thus leaving out women who might not have been fertile, or might not have had heterosexual relations, or might have chosen to limit their reproduction. Our attention focuses like a lens on only one aspect of experience, preventing us from seeing other activities that may have been more important to the lives of women or men than reproduction.

Difference beyond sex

An exclusive focus on sex may distract us from other features that artists intentionally emphasized when they produced images such as early European figurines. The two-sex model of gender identity constrains even recent discussions of depictions of clothing and body ornaments, based on clues from Dolní Věstonice. Figurines are assigned to one of two dichotomous sexes in the beginning step of these analyses. Other characteristics of individual figurines are automatically absorbed into the definition of two gender categories. All examples of textile patterns on Paleolithic figurines are on figurines otherwise classified as female. Displaying textiles thus becomes a generalized characteristic of being female in Paleolithic Europe, and could easily be seen as another attribute of the Great Goddess. But most Paleolithic female figurines do not display textiles. Having textiles is not itself a characteristic of being female, but of being a certain kind of person, distinct from otherwise similar persons who could be assigned to the same sex category. When we begin with gender identity, we predetermine the significance of characteristics: we look for what is shared, and take those things that are shared, even in part, as evidence of gender identity. We need to consider differences within the group of female figurines to be as important as identities among them.

What would happen if we did not begin by assigning figurines to one of two sexes? Then we might carry out an analysis that first divided figurines into those with and without textiles, since this is one of the most visually distinctive features of these figurines. Within the group with textiles, we would observe that the kinds of textiles depicted vary depending on the region where the figurines were made. By implication different textiles were made and used for items of clothing in local areas. We could produce our entire analysis without ever interpreting textiles as attributes of one sex. This would allow us to note that among the very small number of identified male figurines, there is one with a possible representation of a textile. This single example of a male with a textile should call into question the procedure of dividing figurines by sex and associating textiles with one sex.

We might still make the argument that women were textile specialists, based on ethnographic analogy. But this argument would have to be based not on the fact of female sex, but on other factors. These might include the roles women are thought to have had in hunting and gathering in a society with a diverse economy, roles that might have provided them with opportunities to test different materials and discover which worked well for producing textiles.

Instead of simply being a characteristic of all women, the specific kinds of work that might have led some women to experiment with fibers could be seen as a basis for difference among women as much as for identification between them. The value attributed to products of textile arts then would come into focus as a possible source of prestige for individual women and their social relations, not a general characteristic of women as a class.

In this kind of approach, the social motivation for creating figurines becomes a question, in contrast with the all-purpose answer provided by the identification of figurines as images of a goddess or records of female fertility. Paleolithic European figurines recorded uneven participation in the use of textiles. By visibly recording textile use, they opened up to discussion (in the past as much as in the present) differences not of sex – since by the criteria applied, most figurines are of a single sex – but in terms of other kinds of individual and group distinctions.

In the European context, not assuming that gender identity is the question of most interest allows us to see evidence of social differences in the lives of very early ancestral humans. The urgency for an alternative to simple models of gender identity based on the dichotomy of sex is even greater in archaeological studies elsewhere. Norms of gender in Native American societies often did not conform to a simple dichotomy. Archaeologists working on Native American sites have investigated issues of gender identity and difference in societies where a two-sex/two-gender model is clearly inadequate. Their work in turn can transform how we think about the experience of sex, even in societies where at first glance the two-sex/two-gender model seems to be applicable.

Gender difference in Native North America: Beyond dichotomies

He was with us a year or two and always spoken of as a boy by us and by the Inds. [Indians]. *After a time he began to wear the 'Petone'* [bidonne] *or large square of cloth over the shoulders* [a traditional article of women's clothing] *and was in great demand at grinding bees and other female activities in the village. In another year he had quite an illness it appeared and came to tell me of it, and that he could not work for me any longer .... I did not see him at all that winter but in the spring* [of 1890] *a camping party which included Dr. Fewkes came to Zuni and hired Quewishty as cook and he came out in full female attire.*[13]

This is how Mary Dissette, who lived at Zuni pueblo in New Mexico in 1888, described changes in the apparent gender of Kwiwishdi, a Zuni she knew from childhood. In North America, historical accounts, ethnographies, oral narratives, and first-person biographical accounts repeatedly describe individuals whose biological sex would have required them to be assigned to one gender category in a two-sex model, but whose activities and dress affiliated them with another.[14]

Archaeologists working on sites in North America thus confront serious problems created by using a simple two-sex model of gender identity. Researchers coming from societies in which a firmly fixed two-sex/two-gender model exists have exceptional difficulty even finding ways to talk about societies such as Zuni, in which there are more than two genders, or lives like those of Kwiwishdi, whose gender changed over a lifetime, without portraying these people as violations of norms, as transgressive, alternative, or otherwise exceptions to a presumably natural, universal, system of two sexes corresponding to two genders. Struggling to find ways to recognize gendered experiences that provide more than two socially accepted ways of being a sexed person, scholars have had to examine the ways they speak about gender and the relations they assume should ordinarily exist between biological sex and social experiences.

This has been especially the case because most ethnographic accounts emphasize the strength of sexual divisions of labor in Native American societies, with women and men carrying out distinct, often complementary, activities.[15] One of the most common ways anthropologists became aware of individuals who did not fall into the either/or classification of male and female was when a man or woman carried out activities that the ethnographer thought were definitively assigned to people of the other sex. But these observations did not automatically call into question the dichotomous model of sex; they simply suggested some individuals identified across gender lines. Reconsideration of ethnographic and historic evidence questioned initial interpretations of these cases as cross-identification with one of two discrete genders. It is much more consistent with the historic and ethnographic descriptions to think of gender in these native North American societies not in terms of two sexes, but in terms of a broader range of ways of acting as a sexed person.

Archaeologists today explore how the experiences of people in some Native American societies were organized so that more than two sex/gender positions were produced.[16] To accomplish this, a big problem with the original archaeological approach to identifying gender, finding residues of tasks assigned to women and those carried out by men, had to be faced. In societies where so-called "third gender" individuals lived, a division between men and women's work may simply not be valid if, as historical accounts suggest, these people undertook a mixture of tasks, and wore clothing that incorporated items otherwise worn by both men and women. In some cases, such individuals – often called "two-spirit people" following the lead of a group of indigenous scholars – were said to out-perform women or men in tasks defining sex/gender statuses. The potential for incorrectly identifying people as women or men, based on the products of or residues from the superlative work of someone whose underlying biology did not meet the scholar's models, served as a warning that the basic two-sex/two-gender model itself was not a reliable framework for archaeology in native North American sites. Many archaeologists took this as an opportunity to revise the way they thought about sex/gender systems and how they approached archaeological sites.

Deeper understanding: How ideas develop over time

In a series of studies, bioarchaeologist Sandra Hollimon developed a new way of thinking about sex in native Californian sites.[17] Her first studies accepted the approach of looking for "signatures" for men and women, patterns of associations specific to two groups. So she proposed that native Californian cemeteries should have distinct patterns of treatment of the majority of males and of females. She expected there to be a few people buried in some way that was different from the people with whom they shared biological sex, marking them as third-gender people.

The archaeological evidence confronted Hollimon with a real puzzle. She had begun by looking at historic accounts of the frequency and activities of two-spirit individuals to develop her expectations for their burial treatment. The problem was that the burials she found did not conform to these expectations. For example, among the Chumash who lived around Santa Barbara, California, the focus of her study, two-spirit men were compensated for their work with baskets, which were the products of craft work by women. But when Hollimon tried to use presence/absence of baskets to identify men with a third-gender identity, she found that male and female skeletons were equally likely to have baskets. She realized that mortuary analyses are only useful as reflections of gender difference if the living survivors take steps to discriminate between different genders in death. An apparent "contradiction" between biological sex and treatment of the dead (including objects placed in burials) is only informative about the person buried if the survivors are motivated to commemorate the differences that existed in life. Despite being products of women's work among the Chumash, baskets were not placed in the burials of women any more often than in the burials of men.[18]

Hollimon found a more promising avenue of potentially identifying third-gender males, who carried out the same work as most women, by looking at patterns of skeletal deterioration that resulted from repetitive movements. She identified two skeletons of males who died at a young age, whose patterns of spinal arthritis were different from the other male skeletons. Spinal arthritis like this was typical of females. Hollimon explained this skeletal alteration as the result of repeatedly using digging sticks, which placed stress on the spine. This was a typical task of Chumash women.

Both of the young males with this pattern of alteration were actually buried with digging stick weights. While other males also had these artifacts in their burials, the same two young men were the only males to have baskets as well. Hollimon noted that Chumash undertakers used these two tools. This was an occupational specialization strongly associated with third-gender people, lending support to the identification of these burials as third-gender individuals. The low frequency of potential third-gender people that she identified, with two among the burials she studied, was comparable to the frequency ethnographers had reported in their observations of historic California Native American societies. Hollimon's study found that patterns in mortuary settings (even if quite low in frequency) could provide real insights into the lives of third-gender individuals.[19]

As her work progressed Hollimon learned more about the role these people played in Chumash society, and began to question the original approach she had adopted, despite the apparent productive outcome.[20] What she had actually identified, she noted, were two good candidates for members of the Chumash undertaking "guild." Chumash people who buried the dead were historically described with the same word ('aqi) used to translate Spanish and English terms for male homosexual. Documentary sources seemed contradictory, some describing these grave diggers as older women, others as third-gender males. Ultimately, Hollimon identified 'aqi as at heart the term for undertakers, not a word for a gender category or sexual identity. In Chumash society, these people helped the spirits of the dead make the transition to their next stage of life. To be able to do this, they needed a special spiritual status. This special status was limited to those whose sexual activity could not lead to childbirth. Eligible people for this calling consequently included men whose primary sexual partners were other men, celibates, and women past menopause. Third-gender individuals – biological males who were distinct in their gender identity from other males – were able to act as undertakers because of the way they lived. In the case of post-menopausal women, *'aqi* identity clearly came after a prior period of a distinct sexual status. Hollimon had another critical realization: Chumash people could be *'aqi* at certain points in their lives instead of permanently having that status. Rather than being a gender identity that was innate and unchanging, the Chumash status was one demarcated by particular kinds of sexual practices.

For this Native American society, gender was linked to sexuality. But this was not simply a case of having two sexes based on the role each played in heterosexual sexuality. It is not even enough to propose that there were three or four genders corresponding to heterosexual men and women, and homosexual men and women. Instead, gender was fluid, the product of specific kinds of actions rather than an innate form of subjectivity. Gender was related to reproduction, but reproduction itself was more than simply fathering or mothering a child. Undertakers had a place in a sophisticated vision of creation in which burial was part of the processes of regeneration of life. Their own sexuality was critical to their ability to mediate this transition for others.

For Hollimon, not finding three burial patterns led to a realization that sex may not have been the most significant basis for the identity of these people even though ethnographers emphasized their sexual and gender identity. The roles that two-spirits had in these California native societies drew on the additional spiritual power they were understood to have. Genders were not permanent categorical identities, but rather distinctive performances related to sexuality that could change over a person's life.

Manly-hearted women and third-gender families

Archaeological studies of Plains and native Californian burials have suggested that some females, whose patterns of traumatic injury match what we might expect from participation in violent combat, were participants in warfare.[21] Starting with what people do, rather than what people are, changes how we look at material traces as clues to gendered lives. The archaeological evidence from the Plains parallels descriptions recorded in documentary history for varied experiences of gender.[22] Here, powerful women such as Running Eagle of the Peigan and Woman Chief of the Crow were described as distinguishing themselves in warfare.[23] These warrior women headed households in which other women, wives in the case of Woman Chief and dependents in the case of Running Eagle, who remained unmarried in response to a vision, carried out work that contributed to their success.

While not warriors, the "manly-hearted women" of the Peigan are another historically documented example of more fluid gender in practice. Outspoken, publicly assertive, ambitious and acquisitive, they built up substantial property of their own. These were ideals more typical of Peigan men. Manly-hearted women excelled in tasks typical of both men and women. They married husbands who departed from the stereotypical expression of Peigan masculinity, who supported their wives in public, and contributed to the household while not contesting the claims of property ownership by their manly-hearted wives. Manly-hearted women could achieve the status of Chief Wife, the highest-ranking wife in households of men with multiple wives, while simultaneously building up their own wealth and public standing in ways more typical of men.

Usually described as exceptions to a rule, individual biographies of warrior women and manly-hearted women exemplify what we should expect in societies with more fluid, less categorical models of gender. Individual girls could strive for achievement in arenas strongly associated with men, provided they had the support of others, their families of birth and the households they formed as adults. The actual traces of these different gendered lives might be in very different places than archaeologists originally thought to look.

Archaeologist Elizabeth Prine realized that archaeologists should be able to identify households of third- or fourth-gender people in the Plains because they would be composed of unusual numbers and proportions of occupants, compared to other houses in a village. Her analysis of an Hidatsa village site along the Missouri River explored this possibility. Here, one among a series of lodges, represented by the patterns left in the soil by their perishable posts, was substantially smaller than the others. It was also distinctively built with double posts where most lodges had single posts (fig. 21).[24] Prine suggested that both the smaller size and the double line of posts were clues that this lodge was constructed and occupied by an Hidatsa two-spirit.

The historic Hidatsa lived in multi-generational households connected through women, in which in-marrying men and unmarried sons lived with mothers, their daughters, and their granddaughters. Sisters routinely married the same man, living together with their in-married husband in the lodge of

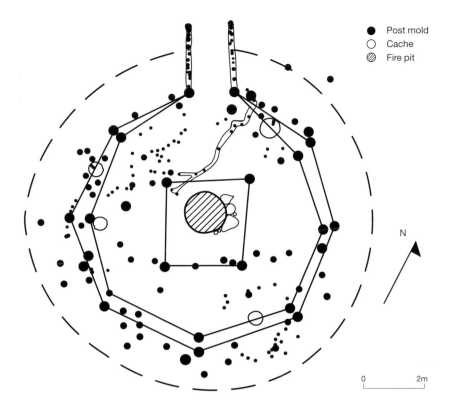

21 Layout of an unusual earth lodge in the Hidatsa site Rock Village, a possible residence of a third-gender person and his/her household.

their mother. The smaller size of the double-post lodge consequently suggests a different kind of family organization with fewer members of the family. Hidatsa two-spirits formed households composed of only an adult couple and their children, and so probably occupied smaller lodges.

Prine associated aspects of the construction of this distinctive lodge itself with its likely use by a Hidatsa two-spirit. Hidatsa two-spirits, biologically male, participated in ceremonies with females, where they carried out tasks that required strength greater than that of biological females. This included raising large posts for the ceremonies, and, Prine suggests, raising posts for construction of earth-lodges. Prine argued that the double row of posts on the unusual small lodge might have had special symbolic meaning, related to the "doubled" nature the Hidatsa attributed to two-spirits. In this analysis, Prine expanded the ways it is possible to "see" gender diversity to encompass evidence of the household, ceremonial, and social life of third-gender people.

Archaeologists studying native North American societies can propose no simple model of features that would allow assignment of individuals to dichotomous male or female categories. In order to make sense of historic and ethnographic texts describing gender as not constrained to a sexual duality, scholars had to reconceptualize gender as a continuum of difference. Rather than two categories to which people were unambiguously assigned, each person could be compared to others in relation to specific actions.

Many factors differentiated people from each other, some of them related to biological sex, but characteristics of identity also cut across each other. Whether or not sex/gender status was pertinent varied from one context to another. Rather than being expressions of existing categories, the activities practiced by different people were the way that their place in relation to others was expressed, produced and reproduced, and could be transformed. What mattered, in terms of social distinctions, in the lives of these people was not necessarily what we might assume based on our own experience in contemporary society.

Revisiting the European Paleolithic and Neolithic

Ayla, the heroine of Jean M. Auel's *Clan of the Cave Bear*, experienced striking confrontations with difference, between men and women, more and less skilled in healing and religion, members of the direct human line or its Neanderthal branch. What difference would it make if, instead of emphasizing categories of gender identity, our archaeology of the Paleolithic started by exploring differences in social relations? The first question we would ask could not be "where are the women (or men)," but would have to be, "where is difference at work between people?" Ayla's fictionalized life is based in part on explorations of Paleolithic European sites by archaeologists. But the picture painted by archaeologists interested in gender is even more complex than the fictionalized story.

Archaeologist Margaret Conkey explores sites of different scales as the settings where groups of varied size came together at distinct points in the year.[25] Her work treats Paleolithic Europeans as people with individual skills and lives. Distinctions between men and women may have existed but were not automatically the most important ones. Conkey notes that when Paleolithic people were in the smaller groups in which they spent most of their time, they would have been individually known to each other through shared histories. Rather than relating to each other as categorically male or female, their interactions would have been based on individual biographies known as a result of these shared histories.

Rather than women being incarnations of an abstract Mother Goddess, a specific woman would have been someone's parent, child, and sibling, the teacher of another person, the maker of textiles, the artist who painted the wall of a cave, the hunter who shared in a kill. None of these roles necessarily required specific biological characteristics, although individual physical traits might have helped a person distinguish herself at some of them, just as the greater strength of Hidatsa two-spirits participating in ceremonies singled them out for specific tasks. Within a small group known intimately to each other, individual distinction is more likely to have been pertinent as a basis for planning and action than abstract identities.

Conkey suggests categorical differences would have mattered in other places, where on occasion multiple groups came together, beyond the household. In these larger gathering places, social groups could not rely on ways of acting toward each other that worked in small-scale, face-to-face settings. Conkey uses artifacts as her clues to differences in Paleolithic people's actions in different sites. Distinctive kinds of objects were produced and discarded at larger gathering sites. The range of activities implied at even a small gathering site suggests a great diversity in activity, and thus opportunities for many forms of distinction among the people gathered there. Associating with people with whom they were not continuously engaged every day, in-gathered Paleolithic people must have established relations of identity and difference through multiple forms of identification, including aspects of age, sex, skill, and experience.

Conkey begins by considering what the materials present in these sites suggest about variation among people. In her own approaches to artifacts such as Paleolithic figurines, she maintains a strong emphasis on the contexts where they were likely made, used, and discarded.[26] She emphasizes the differences between figurines, not the similarities, and that simple methodological change alters the picture. Regional variation in form is much more significant in her analyses than shared features. From her perspective, figurines need to be understood as products of a local society before they are used as evidence in models that homogenize vast regions. Within local societies in Paleolithic Europe, figurines may well have been critical as media for the public assertion of social difference, including gender differences. At the same time, as the fictional Ayla discovers in the books that follow *Clan of the Cave Bear*, differences within a gender, based on local group membership, skill, or family position, may be as important in everyday life as bonds of identity rooted in similar biological experiences.

3

Amazons, queens, and sequestered women:

Gender and hierarchy

In March 1980, I sat in a packed auditorium in Austin, Texas, enthralled like everyone else as art historian Linda Schele led us through a step-by-step method to read the texts inscribed in the seventh and eighth centuries on the walls of temples at Classic Maya Palenque, Mexico. As she taught us to recognize the names of the rulers of Palenque, and to identify the phrases where they named their fathers and mothers, a picture emerged of powerful men – and women who had ruled in their own right, or as regents for their sons and heirs. This was a revolutionary event, the fourth in a series that continues today. Together, we glimpsed the life of a long-dead royal woman from this city-state, daughter of the previous ruler, passing the emblems of rulership on to her own son, who would become the most renowned ruler of the site in its history.[1]

For me, this workshop, and others in which I participated in later years, raised urgent questions. If women were named as rulers in public monuments, then why did archaeologists – then and now – treat women in power as exceptions to a

Classic Maya norm? If women could pass on control of the throne to their sons, then how could we argue that Classic Maya society was strictly patrilineal? The revelations about Maya women in positions of power that flowed in a steady stream in the 1970s and 1980s were evidence that social hierarchy trumped gender hierarchy in this complex society.

Learning to see Classic Maya women

The road to these insights had been long. By 1950, archaeologists working in the cities of Central America had been challenged to move forward from the butterfly collecting of classifying artifacts to try to understand ancient societies.[2] Here, ancestors of the modern Maya, who still inhabit parts of Mexico, Guatemala, Belize, El Salvador, and Honduras, used written texts and visual images – stone sculptures, painted pottery, and clay figurines – to record issues of interest to them during what is now called the Classic Period (ca. AD 250–850). The dominant understanding of these texts and images at mid-century was that Classic Maya texts dealt with religion, astronomy, and divination. The accompanying images were understood to depict male priests and gods.[3] Women were nowhere to be found in these discussions of Classic Maya society. Interpretations of sixteenth-century European texts describing the descendants of some Classic Maya in Yucatan were used as evidence that women had no role in public life, were excluded from religious rituals, and were considered ritually contaminated. Earlier suggestions that some Classic Maya images showed women were rejected or simply ignored.[4]

Then, in the 1950s and 1960s, Tatiana Proskouriakoff began to question the assumption that political life was unrecorded in Maya art. Proskouriakoff was an artist who had worked with some of the major Maya archaeological projects. She compared Classic Maya society to European states ruled by noble families, and explicitly assumed that Maya noblewomen were among those pictured in images and recorded in texts.[5] Her pioneering work would inspire other scholars to re-evaluate the role of elite Maya women.

Proskouriakoff began by analyzing monuments from one Classic Maya site, Piedras Negras, in spatial and chronological context. At this site, groups of monuments had been set up in lines in front of individual buildings. Proskouriakoff observed that each group of monuments, which could be dated precisely using the Maya calendar, covered a period of time within the possible lifespan of a human being. In each group, she saw that the earliest dates were found with distinctive visual motifs and signs in the as-yet undeciphered Maya writing system.

On these earliest monuments in each set she identified an "ascension motif" that showed a seated figure, often on a platform at the top of a ladder. Proskouriakoff suggested that this was a record of the assumption of the throne by a new ruler, and that each set of monuments was the product of one reign. Rather than being concerned with esoteric religious and astronomical affairs, she suggested that Maya monuments were records of the lives of kings and queens.

Her re-introduction of women as a subject of Classic Maya art and texts was equally careful and contextually supported by multiple lines of evidence.[6] On monuments with the ascension motif, there was often a second figure shown standing at ground level, looking up toward the figure seated above (fig. 22). These standing figures were dressed in long robes that reached ankles and wrists, and had conventionally been interpreted as specialist priests. Proskouriakoff argued instead that these robes could be compared to women's garments in traditional Maya villages of the twentieth century. She also noticed that when a figure dressed in this fashion was shown on a monument, the text accompanying it often had a particular profile head as a repeated sign. That profile head Proskouriakoff compared to similar signs in

22 Classic Maya Stela 14 from Piedras Negras, showing a person identified as the mother of the ruler standing gazing up at her son.

23 Female figures in Postclassic
Maya Codex Dresden.

codices, the folded books created by Maya in Yucatan many centuries later (ca. AD
1300–1500), several of which were sent to Europe in the sixteenth century and
survived in libraries there. In these Maya Postclassic manuscripts, a similar sign
appeared in captions above human figures shown with carefully depicted female
breasts (fig. 23). The historical context Proskouriakoff traced, from Classic Maya
images and texts on stone sculptures to Postclassic Maya texts and images in
folding books and to the clothing practices of contemporary living Maya,
strengthened her suggestion that the Classic images represented women of the
ruling families whose histories were recorded in the monuments.

Implications of "finding" Classic Maya women

The generations of scholars who followed accepted the direction that Proskouriakoff established, and continue today to identify specifics of the lives of Classic Maya men and women of the ruling class by interpreting texts and images on monuments.[7] In monumental sculpture, images identified as women are less common than those identified as men, a fact established by Proskouriakoff herself, explained as evidence that in Maya politics, power was normally transmitted from fathers to sons. Archaeologist Joyce Marcus, one of Proskouriakoff's students, showed that women were more common in the visual record at smaller sites located near and connected to larger cities.[8] She suggested that ruling families of smaller towns were socially allied to rulers of larger cities through marriages in which daughters traveled from the powerful centers to the smaller courts of less powerful noble families.

Another student of Proskouriakoff, art historian Clemency Coggins, addressed the less common pattern, in which women were prominent in monuments at some of the most powerful Classic Maya cities.[9] Tikal, Guatemala, was at the time thought to be the single largest city of the Maya world. Both texts and images from the early period of the city's history recorded women. Coggins, following Proskouriakoff, suggested these women were in the line of succession of power at Tikal, transmitting the right to rule from their fathers to their sons. Examples of this pattern were not limited to Tikal, and at other sites, including Naranjo and Palenque, the women involved clearly exercised power before their sons took over rulership.

As an exception to what was assumed to be a norm of patrilineal succession, women transmitting the right to rule was seen as a problem. Scholars created speculative historical narratives in which succession to power through women was an exception required in specific instances due to the lack of a male heir. Linguistic anthropologists and archaeologists debated whether instead of a patrilineal system of social relations, the Classic Maya might have instead had more complex kinship systems in which relations could be traced through male and female links.[10] Underlying all these arguments was a shared understanding that also was found in contemporary anthropological studies of gender, which was that women holding power was an anomaly. But if it was such a transgression of social norms, why did Classic Maya rulers install large-scale sculptures that would have continually reminded people of such a serious flaw in their claims to power?

Gender difference and inequality

To most researchers, the mothers of Classic Maya rulers at Palenque and Naranjo were women first, members of ruling families second. Their roles in childbirth and child-rearing were understood to inevitably color their treatment in life. Noting a repeated pattern of economic and political disadvantages suffered by women in many contemporary societies, scholars long struggled to explain why women were ranked lower than men and blocked from equitable access to social resources. Feminist anthropologists writing in the 1970s and early 1980s identified three dualistic contrasts that they felt could be the basis for explanations of such asymmetries along lines of sex.[11] Women's roles in childbirth and child-rearing figured centrally in all of these. Pragmatically, women were assumed to have actual economic disadvantages because of the greater burdens they incurred through pregnancy, birth, and childcare. Men, while claiming paternity, were not subject to the direct physical consequences and were understood to be able to evade direct responsibility for childcare.

Because women were preoccupied with childcare, scholars assumed they were tied more securely to the home base, and thus denied opportunities to participate in life outside the household. The private sphere of childcare and housework was considered subordinate to a public sphere where prestige was achieved and where political debate happened. Men, not tied to the home, were the actors in the public sphere, and women, dependent on men economically, had access to political life and social distinction only through them.

The association of women with child-bearing and child-rearing was also seen as the basis for a symbolic distinction from men. Because menstruation, childbirth, and lactation are biological processes, women, it was argued, were tied more securely to nature. The occupants of the contrasting category, men, were then in a position to be associated exclusively with culture.

More recent gender scholarship has challenged the original empirical claim that men universally were at a political advantage over women, demonstrating that there has been more variation in men's and women's relative status historically and ethnographically, with women having opportunities to achieve high status in many societies. The understanding of even those situations that seemed clear-cut examples of the exclusion of women from influence shows that women may have distinct forms of social power, or different understandings of relative social standing, than men in their societies. When studies of inequality abandon the initial presumptions of a two-sex model, they can even demonstrate that sex/gender may not be the most important basis for identity. They can show how other forms of difference, such as social status, may have distinguished men and women more than sex difference. Archaeologists have been active in making arguments of all of these kinds, exploring the lives of women in power through the material clues they left behind.

Women warriors

Women in mobile Iron Age Central Asian societies dependent on horses capture the imagination as possible real examples of the Amazons of Classical Greek texts. Archaeologist Jeannine Davis-Kimball described material traces of people she called women warriors in tombs from Central Asia, where both biological males and females are buried with weapons and gear for horses.[12] Like women who ruled, women warriors challenge assumptions about women categorically being less powerful than men. Davis-Kimball's work allows us to explore how multiple lines of evidence can be used to support an argument that some women had status equal to that of men.

Davis-Kimball defined categories of objects taken as evidence of the life experiences of those with whom they were buried. These categories of objects

were then compared with the biological sex of the person in each burial. Many different associations were found with women's burials, leading Davis-Kimball to define multiple forms of femininity. These include artifacts associated with traditional feminine tasks, such as spinning, and evidence of religious practices, as well as other objects she recognizes as characteristic of women warriors (fig. 24). The actual distribution of these things is complex, and individual

24 Young woman from Cemetery 2, Kurgan 8, Burial 4 at Pokrova, Russia, buried with a dagger and arrowhead, leading to her identification as a warrior.

burials contained mixtures of them. Some objects, notably those typical of women warriors, were also found in burials of males. Davis-Kimball reaches the conclusion that women enjoyed access to a broader range of statuses than men, and that the highest statuses, which she identifies with religious practice and warfare, were as open to women as they were to men.

But the picture is not quite so simple, nor so easily interpreted as evidence for female domination of prestige and power. The largest tombs, with the greatest amount of material, were of males. In total, 94 percent of the males were buried with objects interpreted as evidence of warrior status. The number of women found with comparable objects is quite a bit smaller. Most women's burials, about 75 percent, instead contained the objects used to define what Davis-Kimball calls "hearth femininity." While press coverage of her work presented the small minority of women associated with weapons as evidence of Amazon warriors, Davis-Kimball actually suggests more specifically that these women probably participated in the defense of herds and home.

So what does this study actually tell us about inequality between men and women? If we treat the evidence according to traditional archaeological approaches, like those used in the studies of Tlatilco described in the last chapter, our first step would be to identify categories of burials with the most rare, exotic, expensive, or greatest number of materials, and graves or tombs that required the most effort to build. From that perspective, the top level of this society was composed of a small number of men. At the other end of the spectrum were graves of men and women with few or no objects included. In between these extremes, the majority of men and women were buried with some objects. One class of objects, weapons and horse gear, was found in the burials of both men and women. Other sets of objects, treated as evidence of "hearth" status or of religious practice, were found only in female burials. It is not clear if there are additional sets of objects that were found only with male burials, partly because almost all male burials contained weapons. Can we interpret the different frequencies of these sets of objects as evidence for the categorical identity and status of men and women? Specifically, does the fact that some women were buried with weapons mean that women, as a category, had special or high status?

The answers we give to these questions depend on assumptions we make about gender and society. If we start with a two-sex model that assumes that every woman's (or man's) experience is related most closely to her (or his) sex, then anything found out about even one woman (or man) applies to some extent to all the other members of the same sex category. So in this example, advocates of matriarchy see women as a category as having more options open to them than men, more routes to achieve prestige and power, including the role of warrior, which is for some reason considered the most powerful role. Meanwhile, advocates of patriarchy use the same logic but emphasize the fact that only men are in the biggest burials, so the top position of power must be masculine. Women with weapons are all treated as exceptions to the rule that reserves powerful roles for men. Because Davis-Kimball proposes that these women probably served as part of local defenses of home and herd, they are viewed by patriarchy advocates as not really removed from the domestic sphere of women, not really in the public sphere of men. The fact that the majority of males with weapons also likely served primarily as defenders of the group, and that the vast majority of men did not occupy large, fancy tombs, is treated as less important; one man's destiny is all men's identity.

When status is more important than sex

As an alternative, we might consider whether sex was really the most significant dimension of social identity and social difference in this population. In a study of burials in Iron Age Europe (ca. 750–450 BC), archaeologist Bettina Arnold faced an even more striking example of the crossing of expected gender categories.[13] A burial at the site of Vix (in what today is France), dating 480–450 BC, was fitted out as a typical warrior's tomb, with weapons and all the metal objects needed for feasting (fig. 25). The person in the tomb, however, was biologically female. The elaboration of this burial placed it in the top rank, so, unlike the Central Asian case, the top level of this society was not, apparently, exclusively male. The question Arnold faced was, did the Princess of Vix actually have the same roles in life as a male of the ruling class? Her answer is maybe – or maybe not.

Burials, archaeologists know, cannot just be treated as time capsules of every-day life. One of the major questions that has to be asked about every society is, how does treatment of the dead relate to the lives of the living? In the 1960s, a number of influential archaeological models were developed to propose that objects in burials reflected the social identity of the living individual. In the decades since then, the situation has been shown to be more complex. Burials are the result of actions taken by living survivors that are consistent with their relationships with the dead person. They may help us understand how the social group viewed the deceased person, but they may also downplay aspects of the person's individual experience. They may as often cover over some dimension of difference entirely as reflect it.

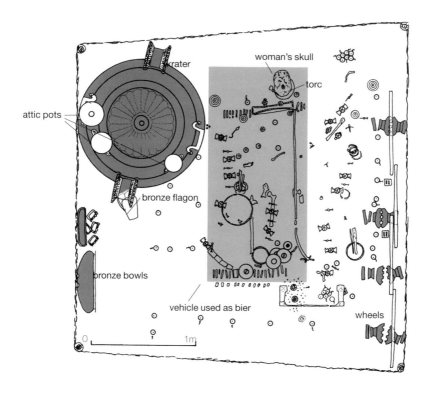

25 Plan of the tomb of the "Princess of Vix" showing the gear associated with her social status.

In the case of the European Iron Age burial at Vix, and others like it, the identification of the buried person with the activities of the high-status group to which she belonged framed the decisions of those who constructed the tomb. Weapons and feasting gear were important to people of that status, including the people who cared enough about this woman to give her a significant tomb. They could even have been so significant that everyone in that status group participated in the use of these objects while alive. The inclusion or exclusion of items from the tomb does not automatically tell us what the person in it did during life. What it does tell us is that there was nothing objectionable to the social group in associating women and men with this suite of activities and objects.

In the Central Asian case, a stronger argument can be made for weapons and horse gear representing the tools actually used by the men and women with whom they were buried. What that tells us is that the lives lived by these people included numerous opportunities that required use of weapons and horses, activities important to the social group and not associated exclusively by them with male or female sex. Some of the women buried with these materials were quite young. It is conceivable that many women had distinct roles at certain points in their lives. Beginning analysis by assuming that variability in burials is primarily about sex difference stops us exploring whether age, family, or status group affiliation might have been a more significant factor in the lives of men and women at this time and place.

Noble women, prestige, and power

In Classic Maya villages, like the one buried and preserved by volcanic ash at Joya del Ceren, El Salvador, rural women's lives took place in the spaces that surrounded the houses where they lived. Most of the lives of Classic Maya queens also were carried out in and around their residences, which were much more lavish in scale, construction, and ornamentation. Yet the differences between the women of Joya del Ceren and those who lived in the palaces of cities such as Palenque or Copán were greater than the similarities between them.

Studies of women's lives in societies with high degrees of difference in social rank make more sense if the women involved are not automatically treated as representative of a single categorical group united with all other women. Texts and images on carved stone monuments, painted on the walls of palaces, and carved and painted on palace luxury goods such as drinking vessels, show Classic Maya men and women of the noble class and ruling houses. Some of the women recorded in these historical media had the same titles as male rulers, and passed on ruling authority to their sons. Others, while not apparently ruling in their own right, participated in the ritual and political life of the courts.[14] Most men and women, though, were not subjects of these kinds of historical records, or appeared in them as unnamed servants and subordinate nobles. Those people are better represented by the other kinds of archaeological traces they left behind: the remains of their houses, the trash they discarded from their everyday existence and the special events that marked their lives. Relatively little excavation has happened in the houses of the farmers who probably made up the majority of the Classic Maya population.[15] Quite a bit more is known about the houses of the non-ruling noble families.[16]

Many of the archaeologists investigating household life among rural farmers and lower-ranking nobles have been explicitly concerned with trying to understand gender relations in Classic Maya society.[17] Rather than see a simple hierarchy of powerful men and less powerful women, these archaeologists redirect our attention to the many ways that people could create and assert prestige in any society that was economically stratified.

In common with most archaeological work on gender, the first explorations of gender relations in Classic Maya households began with a two-sex/two-gender model. In order to explore what men and women were doing in households, archaeologists depended on assumptions about the kinds of tasks each sex carried out. The traces of these different tasks could then provide a way to see men and women in action. Archaeologists working at Classic Maya sites have been particularly explicit about why they see some tasks as typical of men and others as likely the work of women. Along the way, they have also raised much more subtle points about how we can think about men's and women's work in those situations where a social group maintains stereotypes of different roles.

Women's work, women's space

Working at Classic Maya Copán, archaeologist Julia Hendon conducted excavations in a series of households occupied by wealthy members of the nobility who were not part of the ruling family. Among the discarded materials in some, but not all, of the buildings occupied by these groups were tools of textile production. Most distinctive were the whorls that, when attached to spindle shafts, allowed a person to spin thread from native cotton and maguey (a form of agave plant). A series of bone picks, awls, and needles were other tools that could have been used in the kind of weaving known from this region. Hendon was able to demonstrate that both kinds of tools were concentrated near specific buildings, not evenly distributed throughout the sites (fig. 26).

Using evidence from Classic Maya art and later historic and ethnographic descriptions, all of which identified spinning and weaving as stereotypically women's work, Hendon argued that in these specific areas, women were carrying out textile production. She did not claim that all women were engaged in textile production at all times, or that only the places with these tools were sites of women's work. Instead, she emphasized the fact that cloth production was an important part of the Maya economy. Cloth was used for political tribute, and was needed for ritual purposes. The women whose work is hinted at by the tools they used, broke, and discarded were not Everywoman: they were women of powerful families contributing to the economic and political efforts of their family. Hendon suggests that the individual weavers would have been able to

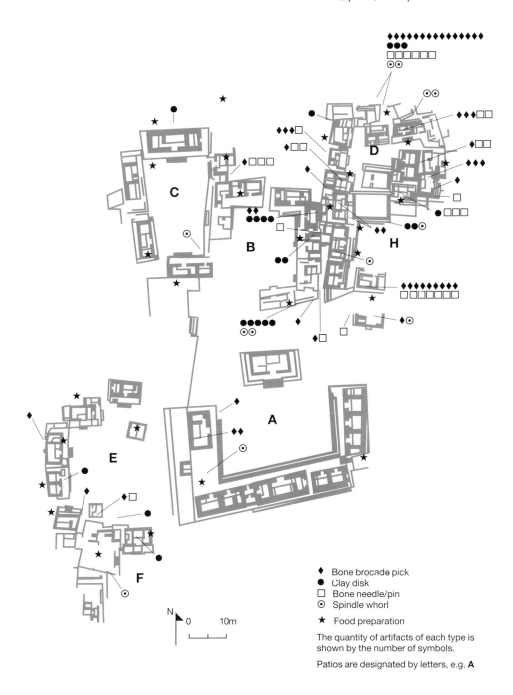

Bone brocade pick
Clay disk
Bone needle/pin
Spindle whorl
★ Food preparation

The quantity of artifacts of each type is shown by the number of symbols.

Patios are designated by letters, e.g. **A**

26 Plan of buildings in noble house compounds at Late Classic Copán, Honduras, showing the distribution of tools used in tasks generally carried out by women.

gain prestige through these efforts. She explicitly argues that production like this, taking place in households, requires us to abandon the division between domestic and public spheres. Women in Copán's noble houses practiced politics whenever they wove cloth for use in ceremonies and rituals.

Hendon and other archaeologists studying Classic Maya society used similar approaches to identify additional sites where women might have been at work, and to suggest that women's work might have been a source of individual prestige and a contribution to the political success of their groups. Food production was another task that historic documents suggested was traditionally the work of women in descendant Maya communities. Grinding the staple grain, maize, required great amounts of labor. Some Maya figurines and painted pottery even showed women grinding corn (fig. 27). *Metates*, the stone grinding platforms, and *manos*, the hand-stones rubbed over the soaked corn kernels, were consequently often used as evidence of areas where women might have been at work. At the rural village of Joya del Ceren, in El Salvador, the eruption of a volcano buried houses and tools rapidly, allowing archaeologists to be certain where grinding

27 Figurine from Late Classic Lubaantun, Belize, showing a woman using a grinding stone.

was taking place and thus where women may have been working. Archaeologist Tracy Sweely used these data to suggest that in this rural village, women's work would have been visible and women would have been in a position to claim credit for their contribution to subsistence and feasting.

Women in private, women in public

These approaches question whether ancient Maya really did divide their space into public and private realms, and directly challenge the assumption that the work that women did in households had no broader public recognition or significance. When misinterpreted, though, this work sometimes was used to support contrary arguments that women were politically marginal and not part of broader public processes. How did this happen?

Some scholars treated the identification of evidence of stereotyped women's labor as the *only* evidence for women's presence. From this perspective, women were only around if there were spindle whorls, weaving tools, or grinding stones. Hendon argued specifically that textile production in noble households was skilled craftwork, with expertise supported in part by the greater economic wealth of the household. Others ignored that point, collapsing noble women into a single sex/gender category with rural women, while treating ruling women named in public monuments as exceptions. So art historian Lynn Ruscheinsky suggested that at Classic Maya Chichén Itzá's Monjas palace, women were excluded from the raised palace itself, forced to work at a platform behind the palace where many grinding stones had been found.[18]

Meanwhile, lintels in the palace were inscribed with the names of the mother and mother's mother of the ruler of the site.[19] Why would that be if women were excluded from the palace itself, and marginalized in royal life? The ruling family at Chichén Itzá traced descent through women, and noble women, like men, were active as patrons of monuments. They are as likely to have walked the halls of the Monjas as the noble men with whom they shared social status and patterns of activity.

Classic Maya Aguateca, Guatemala, is a second case of an interpretation of an archaeological signature for women found in a high-status location in ways that ignore social status and downplay women's potential social importance. Here, rapid abandonment of burned structures preserved luxury craft products in the process of production, as well as the tools used to make them. Some of the tools suggested women's textile skills were being employed in the production of these fancy ornaments. Archaeologist Takeshi Inomata proposed that these women were the wives of the principal craftworkers, men he suggested would have earned whatever credit came from the production of these objects.[20] Even when present in sites where prestigious activities were carried out, women were said not to accrue credit from their own work.

Learning from Classic Maya studies

At least three different issues are raised by the still-lively debates about women in Classic Maya society. First, it is clear that here, as in most other archaeological cases, starting with a two-sex/two-gender model leads to grouping people together (on the basis of sex) who do not really have that much in common. Social standing within Classic Maya society was a much more powerful determinant of people's lives than sex. The lives of royal and noble women were more like those of royal and noble men than like those of rural farming women. The two-sex/two-gender model itself is a historical product of particular times and places. We can force the data into the model, but there will always be contradictions as a result.

Second, it is not impossible to identify actions that are typical of one sex/gender or another, but typical does not mean universal, natural, or uncontested. Not all the things that men and women did at any one time or place were divided along lines of sex. Archaeologist Cynthia Robin powerfully criticizes assumptions made by some scholars that Classic Maya agriculture was a form of work typical of men.[21] Using ethnographic and historic texts and archaeological data from a farming village in Belize, Chan Nohol, she shows that how Classic Maya people historically conducted farming was quite variable. Farming was not men's work; it was work shared by men and women. Stereotyped associations of certain kinds of work with one sex, like the representations of Classic Maya women grinding corn and weaving cloth, are themselves part of the way that gender distinctions are created. These differences may be limited to specific times and places, and even to certain social strata.

Third, if a dichotomy on the basis of sex is taken as automatically the basis of a hierarchy of power and status, then the two-sex/two-gender model will always reproduce stratification by sex. For many scholars, even though there is clear evidence that some women in Classic Maya cities were politically powerful, women as a group are assumed to have been disadvantaged relative to men as a group. Showing that there was a queen or two is not a good way to challenge the kind of thinking that tries to say that women have always been subordinate to men, and by implication, will always be.

Gender inequality and gendered practice

The Classic Maya are widely acknowledged to have allowed noble women to play significant political roles, including in war and ritual, while Classical Greece has been presented as a society where men monopolized public life and economic and political power. Women were legally subjected to their fathers and later to their husbands, and were expected to remain sequestered in private precincts within their houses. The material clues that archaeologists follow contradict the neat picture provided by documentary evidence. A better way to begin to challenge the two-sex/two-gender model is exemplified by archaeologists working on Classic Greek society.[22]

Archaeological studies of household space in ancient Greek cities in fact illustrate that the ideal of sequestration of women was often violated in reality. Re-interpreting social relations within households in terms of a concern with controlling the presence of outsiders better accounts for the data sometimes used to argue that women were confined within the house.

The development of household archaeology is actually relatively recent in Classical archaeology. Most buildings in Greek cities were excavated using methods very different from those that allow archaeologists to specify where different activities were carried out in Classic Maya houses. The association of discarded tools with rooms or sectors of rooms is not always clear. Collection and analysis of microscopic residues is uncommon. What Classical Greek household archaeology has to work with is primarily the plans of buildings, rooms, and city streets. Here there is little emphasis on finding "signatures" of men and women. The expectations about where men and women were in these houses come primarily from documents.

Classical archaeologists can draw on a rich tradition of analysis of texts that stretches back centuries. Many of these are literary or philosophical, offering, among other things, specific commentaries on the nature of men and women. Classical archaeologists also draw on visual documents, the abundant paintings that ornamented pottery used in ceremonies, feasts, and formal meals. These record moments in the lives of generalized women, mythical heroines, and goddesses.

Based on these kinds of documents, Classical scholars believe that women were understood to be fundamentally different from men, not as opposites, but as two degrees of development of the same potential.[23] This one-sex/two-gender model saw women as an inferior version of men, with genitalia that were identical in structure but less developed due to women's essentially lower level of vital energy. Not only were women categorically lesser; young men, foreigners, and adult men who were not citizens were also understood to be less, not just different.

Women of the families of free men were specifically vulnerable to abuse, and the men of their families were to protect them by keeping them out of contact with outsiders. Other women could circulate more freely, including enslaved women serving free women, and women engaged in the sex trade. Here, as with other cases discussed above, it is clear that there was no single category "woman" that could provide guidance for our historical understanding, even though there was an explicitly developed two-gender model.

With the idea that women (meaning women of free citizen families) were sequestered as part of their models, Classical archaeologists have looked at house plans and found evidence of women's quarters.[24] Classical houses in cities such as

28 Plan of a house in Athens showing two ways to understand division of space. On the left, the *andron* is singled out as a room for men to use, separate from other areas of the house where women could circulate. On the right, the striped area is where visitors from outside the house could enter, and the dotted area is the private space of the family.

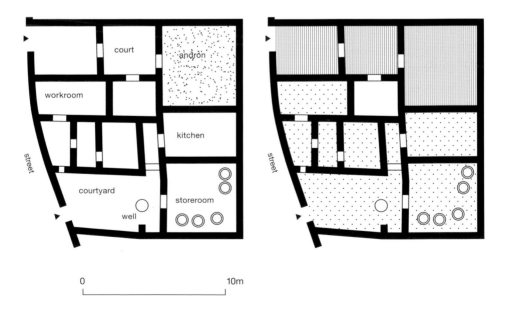

Athens usually had a transitional space opening out onto the street separated from most of the living quarters (fig. 28). They often had a banqueting hall slightly farther into the house. Based on documents, this space was understood to be the place where male members of the house entertained male visitors, while the women of the house stayed in their more restricted quarters. The "women's quarters" made up the most private part of the house, most removed from the entryway and separated from the mixed banqueting hall.

Classical archaeologist Marilyn Goldberg questioned this interpretation. Re-examining house-plans, she showed that this idealized model is less common than one that maintained a two-part separation of reception space and household space. Looking at the data for activities carried out in different sectors of houses, she showed that most of the lives of men of the household also would have been spent in the more private quarters. Houses with formal banquet rooms were unusual, not typical. Rather than an architectural expression of the attempt to control women by secluding them in the house, Classical Greek house-plans protected the privacy of the family while providing a place for the family to interact with outsiders when necessary.

Work like this suggests that in order to make progress we need to abandon the quest for women in the past and the two-sex/two-gender model it brought with it. It is clearly the case that women in many different societies were powerful, successful, distinguished, and recognized for that distinction. It is also clear that the majority of women and men in most ancient societies were not in positions of absolute power and authority. Men and women lived their lives in positions as constrained or determined by their economic wealth, skill, age, and other kinds of identity as by their sex. What archaeologies of gender have had to do is start to directly address questions of the relations that exist between people based on similarities and differences in biological sex and understandings of these similarities and differences at specific times and places. How archaeologists do that is the subject of the following chapters.

4

Sensuous figures, celibates, and sex-workers:

Thinking about sex in the past

S cattered around over 2,000 different locations across Sweden is the largest collection of depictions of the human figure from Bronze Age northern Europe known to scholars. They include representations of armed figures with erect penises. Other figures with long hair and cup marks taken as symbolic of female genitalia have been interpreted as women. Scenes with pairs of figures have been assumed to show a man and woman having sexual intercourse.

It might seem a self-evident conclusion that the ancient Scandinavians who created these images considered distinguishing between males and females to be enormously important, that perhaps sex was the most important distinction in that distant society. Archaeologist Tim Yates studied the entire collection of images and came to very different conclusions. What if, Yates asked, we do not make the prior assumption that the figures represented two categories, warrior men and unarmed women? Could examination of different features of the images lead to entirely new conclusions?[1]

In 1993, Yates published one of the first articles on gender in archaeology that took masculinity as its focus instead of femininity. The material evidence he used was visual: a series of over 2,500 groups of designs carved into bedrock. Dated by most authorities as created between 1800 and 500 BC, the designs represented ships, footprints, animal figures, and human figures (fig. 29). Human figures were by no means the most common subject of representation: that place belonged to ships, which were found in twice the number of rock-art groups as any other motif. But the number of human figures, the second most common motif, made this the largest number of human figures from the time period in the rock art of northern Europe.

29 Bronze Age rock art from Bohuslan region, Sweden.

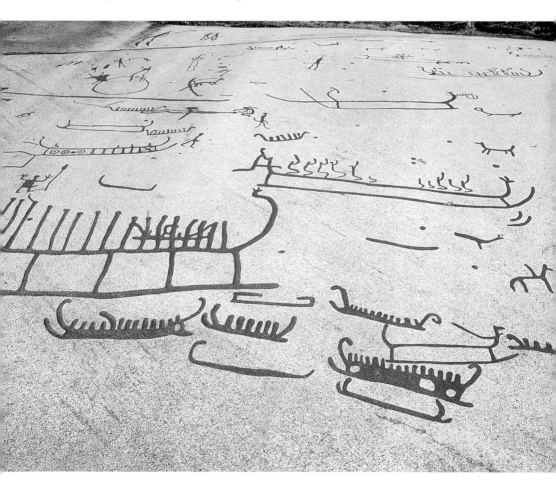

Yates defined his goal as exploring the way that the human body, and in particular, its sexual status, was represented. He recognized four ways the human body was repeatedly represented: unarmed figures; unarmed figures wearing a sword in its sheath; armed figures, defined as those holding a weapon in hand, with a sheathed sword; and armed figures without a sheathed sword. Independent of this general patterning, he tracked whether the figures had features he identified as an erect penis, sometimes with testicles; depiction of muscles in the lower leg; depiction of hands or fingers; horned helmets; or long hair. His analysis of the co-occurrence of the basic types of figures and these additional visual elements found that armed figures with an erect penis were twice as common as figures without explicit depiction of the penis. The figures without depiction of male genitalia were four times as likely to be unarmed. The kinds of weapons found with these two body types also varied, with swords and spears being more common or only found with figures with explicit genitalia. Either kind of figure was equally likely to hold an axe, and figures without genitalia were slightly more likely to hold bows. Helmets were more likely to be depicted on figures with genitalia. While emphasis on hands and fingers did not vary, explicit calf muscles were more common on figures with a clearly depicted penis. Within individual groups of designs, two-thirds of the time those with genitalia were depicted larger than those without. This tendency was even more marked when the comparisons were restricted to figures shown armed and with erect penis, images Yates described as "representatives of the aggressive masculine ethic." These were always larger than other figures with which they were grouped.

Many of the contrasts that Yates drew can be seen as binary: figures with and without a suggestion of a penis; with and without helmets; with and without weapons. Rather than viewing any of these contrasts as evidence of a dichotomy between males and females, he instead took as his beginning point an assumption that there were multiple forms of masculinity in this society. He rejects the possibility that any of these are images of women. He notes that previous studies defined long hair, a cup mark between the legs, and lack of weapons as features of females. He shows that long hair is as likely to be found with phallic figures as with those without markers of presumed male sex. Cup marks were also equally likely to be found with either type of body.

Perhaps most interesting, Yates shows that the major argument used to suggest that non-phallic, unarmed figures are women is a series of images of pairs of figures joined together by entwined arms and bodies (fig. 30). These are

30 Pair of human figures in Bronze Age rock art from Bohuslan region, Sweden.

interpreted as images of sexual intercourse between a phallic male and a non-phallic female. As he notes, the interpretation is a projection of contemporary assumptions about gender roles. He reviews features the non-phallic figures in each pair have in common with other figures likely to be males, such as exaggerated calf muscles, and notes the existence of other paired figures, both human and animal, in which both are phallic. His conclusion is that archaeologists have been operating with a bias toward heterosexual interpretations of human imagery. In his attempt to avoid reproducing this bias, Yates suggests archaeologists consider that the people who created these images may have been more interested in other contrasts than male and female. The more masculine figures are not just male, but male warriors. They are distinguished from other figures that may be either male or female, but above all are not aggressive. From this perspective, the sculpting of muscular calves may be as significant a way of creating bodily difference as the depiction of "primary" sexual characteristics, letting viewers in the past know that the more masculine figures were stronger, muscular, in contrast to the majority of people, whether men or women.

How to stop taking heterosexuality for granted

In the Central Mexican Aztec or Mexica state, the first society in Central America to experience Spanish invasion, most young men were expected to spend years as members of a warrior group. Their prowess as warriors was celebrated and publicly marked in many ways. Some could choose to remain permanently associated with the warrior houses. While warriors, they were not expected to marry or have children. Their primary identification was with their brothers in arms. To understand Mexica society, we need more concepts of masculinity than the two-sex model would provide us.[2]

Tim Yates was struggling with one of the hardest points in contemporary gender studies, the effects on researchers of the most basic assumption about sex: that because sexual relations between (some) biological males and (some) biological females results in offspring, sex is naturally heterosexual. In the years since 1993, the scope of archaeological gender studies has expanded from its initial focus on women's roles and status to include wider considerations of sexuality, including same-sex relationships. Archaeological research now provides many cases of representation of sexualities that cannot be easily encompassed under a two-sex/two-gender model. But it is still the case that researchers often carry forward unquestioned this core assumption. To begin to move ahead, we need to understand what harm is done when analyses begin by assuming the heterosexual perspective.

Anthropologist Kath Weston, among others, has critiqued the two-sex model as inherently *heteronormative*, taking heterosexuality as natural and hence the norm.[3] Even though Weston could document a vast increase in published anthropological studies of same-sex relations from the beginning to the end of the twentieth century, most studies simply described other societies without ever questioning beginning assumptions. Weston drew attention to the fact that most of this research implicitly took the position of a heterosexual researcher. Main questions explored ethnographically were about the tolerance of the heterosexual majority for sexual practices that were "deviant." Ethnographic studies of institutionalized same-sex relations, like those of Native American societies, too often were couched in such a way that they presented same-sex relations as exotic and abnormal, from the perspective of an implicitly heterosexual writer.

Weston drew specific attention to the tendency to lose the historical and particular context in anthropological generalizations. She pointed out that using "man" and "woman" as if they were universally relevant, binary terms that completely described local understandings of sex was unwarranted. The reliance on the very vocabulary of a two-sex model guaranteed reproduction of the model. A biological male wearing clothing like that of women could be seen only as a male passing for female, not as a third sex. An older male having sex with a young boy could be seen only as an erotic relationship, ignoring local explanations about the circulation of semen between male bodies as a key action in reproduction.

Giving up on two-sex models

When archaeologists use a two-sex model, our descriptions of ancient societies, even ones with very different sexual practices, still take for granted that there are only ever two natural, dichotomous sexes defined by reproductive roles. Archaeology can make serious challenges to assumptions like this.[4] First, we have to recognize that our interpretations are impeded by the unconscious logic of the two-sex model. These models lead archaeologists to ignore differences in the life experiences of people whose only similarity is having the same external genitalia. They lead us to misunderstand the real differences of other societies from our own, in such things as their understandings of reproduction and identity.

The two-sex model projected into the past allows archaeologists to approach all ancient societies as if every man and woman was normally a participant in sexual reproduction, something that was not necessarily the case even for men and women engaged in heterosexual relations. Many physical circumstances affect individual fertility; people have long been engaged in controlling the outcomes of sexual relations to avoid pregnancy or to terminate unwanted pregnancies; and in many societies, social barriers existed to limit who was allowed to engender children.

The assumption that only heterosexual relationships were accepted and normal in ancient societies can cause archaeologists to consider as abnormal or socially unacceptable forms of relationship that were, in fact, normal and accepted. In Classical Greek society, older men formed affective and sexual relationships with youths that were the subject of approving representations in both text and visual media. Archaeologists who do not realize the bias they have in favor of the two-sex/two-gender heterosexual model may take same-sex relations in the past as evidence of transgression of a heterosexual norm, when such a simple correspondence between two sexes and two genders may not have existed.

In many instances sexual relations were not fixed exclusively on one kind of person, or varied with age, social status and other factors. The relations that men had with each other in Classical Greece were expected to change with age, and did not preclude affective and sexual relations with women. While Mexica youths were expected to identify with each other in their warrior status, they were encouraged simultaneously to engage in sexual activities with a group of young women who were approved to act as sex partners, free from the obligations of reproduction for their social groups. If they did not decide to remain lifelong warriors, they might make a transition to marriage and a life of fatherhood. Nor did all Mexican youths follow either of these paths. Some were dedicated early in life by their parents to serve as celibate priests in the temples of the gods. The lives of boys who entered temples were more like those of girls dedicated to similar service than they were like the lives of young warriors or fathers with whom male priests shared bodily sexual characteristics. Nor did all boys and girls in Mexica society conform to one of these socially sanctioned ways of living their sexual lives. Texts admonishing wayward boys and girls, and threatening them with bad ends, show that Mexica authorities were concerned that young men and women might engage in same-sex relations, denying the state and their elders offspring to serve as a labor force.[5]

Giving up the two-sex model opens up a much broader range of possibilities in thinking about past societies. It requires us to seek a position that critically examines the things people today think are natural, and can provide a stable beginning point for approaching materials from past societies. The resulting practice of archaeologies of sex and gender is much less straightforward. Where it takes us will often be unexpected. But it does not require the kinds of rich written texts that are available for Classical Greece or the Mexica. Changing our perspective makes more things potential clues to experiences of sex in the past.

The warrior's beauty and the weaver's skill

In European Bronze Age societies, some individual males were buried with weapons, the goods required for drinking alcohol, and other objects used to maintain bodily appearance, such as tweezers. A traditional archaeological approach to mortuary analysis would be to look at objects such as weapons and assign the people with them to one of two categories dictated by the two-sex model. Archaeologist Paul Treherne paid attention to what these objects could tell him about the values important in life to the person buried. The objects in these burials did not simply identify maleness. Instead, they created a picture of the lives of warriors in which masculine beauty was valued. Warrior men were not just everyday men: they were men whose bodies were carefully shaped in life and who continued to be well regarded in death.[6]

In analyses like this, much larger numbers of objects found discarded or included in structured deposits in archaeological sites become clues for sex/gender identities. There is a significant difference between the way Treherne uses these objects as evidence, and previous archaeologists who sought "archaeological signatures" of men and women. These weapons and razors are not traces of a pre-existing male identity. Instead, the actions undertaken by different people in Bronze Age Europe using things found in burials would have produced a sense of being different from each other, and like some others. Action produces a sense of being, rather than simply reflecting something already there. Taking care of their bodies was a part of the warriors' experience that could distinguish them not only from women, but from other men.

Many analyses in contemporary archaeology explore relationships between particular ways of acting and experiences of gender. For scholars studying Classic Maya women's lives, the significance of participation in textile production or maize grinding goes beyond any categorical assignment of tasks to men and women.[7] Noble women spun fine cotton thread at Copán and other cities, and wove fine cloth patterned with symbols of the gods and ancestors from this thread. The cloth Classic Maya women produced was presented to overlords as tribute, was used in ritual offerings, and was converted into the lavish costumes worn by noble men and women. The very tools used while weaving were products of skilled craftwork, decorated with symbols associating the weaver with supernatural patrons. Producing textiles was a part of enacting gender, a gender performance reinforced as valued by images in circulation and by the events where textiles were used. Actions and representations worked together to promote certain ways of being male and female, and presumably also to discourage other ways of acting that were considered inappropriate.

Performing gender

When Classic Maya noble women produced especially luxurious textiles employing carefully crafted and decorated tools, they were not just performing femininity: they were performing a femininity of the noble class. When other people respond with approval, habitually acting in a particular way comes to be experienced as right. The performance of gender may be fore-grounded in some times and places, but it is not the only aspect of being that is subject to enactment and social response. Nor can gender be separated in practice from other aspects of personhood.

Such performances of gender are not innate, but are products of learning and practice. Learning to act in a specific way begins in childhood, and different aspects of performance cannot be separated from each other. The sixteenth-century hybrid documents produced by the Mexica of Central Mexico after the Spanish invasion include textual and visual stereotypes of action appropriate for boys and girls of different ages (fig. 31). The growing girl gradually gained expertise in spinning and weaving. These actions embodied her aging into adulthood as much as they did her performance of one form of femininity.[8]

Gendered performances like these are literally written in the bones, where bioarchaeologists can reveal the habitual activities undertaken by ancient peoples through examination of the traces of muscles attachments, patterns of degenerative arthritis, and other alterations to the bone caused by activity during life.[9] These traces are clues to changes in the way gender was performed over time. In sites occupied before European contact in the southeast United States, skeletal traces of intensive labor increase over time for both males and females, with differences in the specific areas of the skeleton affected suggesting that what women and men did became more differentiated over time.[10] In a comparison of

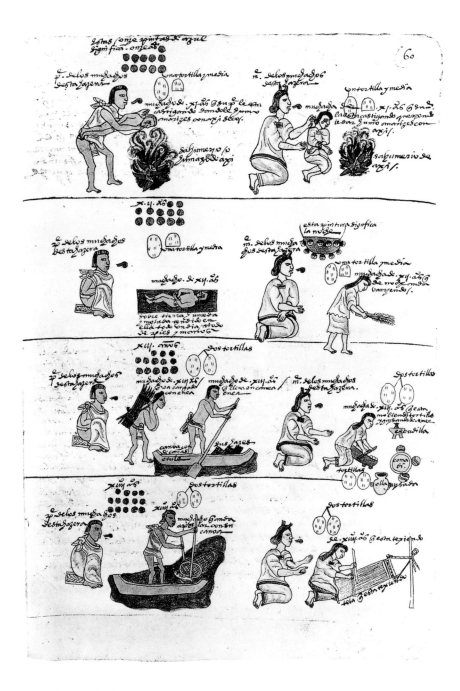

31 Mexica boys and girls age eleven through fourteen being instructed by adults in work appropriate to their age and sex.

two sites in Kentucky, one before and one after the adoption of farming, all indications suggest that women's workload increased, while men's either stayed the same or decreased. A parallel study of sites in Illinois also found that with the new practice of farming, women's skeletons were affected by more work than before. In this study, men's level of labor stayed the same, but based on changes in where bone deteriorated, the activities men carried out were transformed. The last two studies might suggest that women everywhere in the southeast US worked harder once farming came into vogue, but other studies found the opposite. With the introduction of agriculture at the Dickson Mounds site in Illinois, both men and women showed more evidence of heavy work, but here, the new work introduced was more burdensome for men.

Bioarchaeologists sometimes can interpret the clues they see on human skeletons as evidence of specific actions. A study of the California Chumash found that in early sites, men and women had similar levels of wear on their bones, but in different areas.[11] Men's shoulders, elbows, and hands were more affected, while women showed the effects of work in their knees and spines. These differences could be related to women using digging sticks and grinding stones, while men carried out other tasks with tools that called on the use of their shoulders and arms. In this study, again, changes were evident over time. In later sites, men and women had similar patterns of deterioration, at a time when historical documents suggest men and women participated in the same range of tasks.

Not all skeletons sexed as female or male in Native American sites conform to the same patterns of activity. Even when stereotyping of work roles by sex exists, the range of variability never completely corresponds to a two-sex model.[12] When Native American two-spirits carried out skilled crafts also practiced by men or women, they performed their gender in a way that cannot be reduced to one of two sexes. Archaeological investigations profit from leaving the question of "how many sexes" behind in favor of direct consideration of how people in the past lived their embodied lives, and how different forms of embodied action were encouraged or discouraged.

Beautiful bodies, sexual performances

In idealized performances of gender recorded in paintings on Classic Maya pottery, young men engaged in dancing and playing ball display their bodies in front of audiences of older men and women. Pots made for serving food and drink, painted or carved with pictorial scenes like these, were among the most widely admired objects produced in the courts of Classic Maya rulers and nobles.[13] Many of the intact pots found in museums and illustrated in art books were recovered in illegal excavations and exported against the laws of their countries of origin, destroying clues that might otherwise have been used in their interpretation. Some have been excavated by archaeologists, as have vast amounts of fragments from broken pots. Residues of chocolate drinks have been identified in many pots, supporting the captions painted or carved on them that identify the foods they were made to contain.[14] It is clear that each court used many of these pots for feasts and for everyday meals. They were also often placed in the tombs of the highest-ranking families. The imagery they carry would have been pervasive in the lives of the ruling social group. What was selected for representation incorporated the values of this group.

What was represented also served as a model against which individual living action was interpreted. This is a familiar experience for us today. Contemporary controversies swirl around the influence photographs of dangerously thin fashion models can have on girls and women. These images present idealizations of the body that serve as models against which women evaluate themselves, and that they strive to approximate, sometimes at great cost. Similarly, the visual media that circulated in Classic Maya courts provided precedents recreated by living people in their own performances of gender, models against which they must have measured themselves.[15] I decided to study how images like these, circulating in Classic Maya cities provide evidence for the ways in which Maya men and women formulated and indeed reformulated gender identities.[16]

I began with an attempt to move beyond the correspondence model of sex and gender, because it was clear from even a cursory review of sixteenth-century texts that indigenous people in Mexico and Central America understood gender to be more variable than could be captured by two dichotomous sexes. Texts talked about supernatural beings who encompassed male and female aspects, or who were male and female at different points in time. This kind of variability, part of what art historian Cecelia Klein has characterized as gender ambiguity, was routinely associated with positions of political power.[17] Some male officials in Classic Maya and sixteenth-century Mexica societies appeared to cross-dress, wearing items of clothing understood to be normal for women.

I wondered if the imagery used in Classic Maya art could show how indigenous people could take on multiple gender identities in the same way that these later texts did. Initially, I assumed that sex was a biological reality, and gender was a social construct through which sex was interpreted. This was the idea of sex and gender current in archaeology in the early 1990s, but it soon became clear that this approach led to results that simply did not match the way that the ancient Maya led their lives. Why force the lives of these people into a straitjacket of notions invented by late twentieth-century societies? Once I began to try to understand the gender identities of the Maya on their own terms, I realized that visual media could be considered as active, part of the way concepts of gender were given a sense of naturalness, rather than as passive reflections of something that simply existed. Gender was a work in progress, it was something people did, not something people were. Representations were part of the material that people employed as they performed their own gender and as they shaped the gendered experiences of others.

I now see my first attempts at gender analysis as compromised by the two-sex model. Separating sex out as "real" makes it easy for critics to suggest that gender is "unreal," that it does not come to terms with the realities of people's lives, let alone the "given" of biological sex. But even with this initial flaw, adopting a concept of gender that was not predetermined as dual and that did not automatically group all males together and separate them from a second category of females proved to be a useful way to start my analysis, as it was for many other researchers.

Steps to sex in Classic Maya archaeology

Initially, I examined Classic Maya stereotyped images in monumental sculpture and painting as precedents for the actions of women, men, and persons of alternate genders. I compared what was being represented in these media with painted and carved pots and fired clay figurines, produced in molds or modeled by hand, recovered from house compounds. I quickly realized that I needed to specify that the kind of womanhood and manhood I was disentangling was specific to the noble sector of society. Very little archaeological exploration had been carried out in the houses of rural farmers or the more modest residences in cities. Where such work had happened, visual images of any kind were quite rare, suggesting that the way gendered personhood was shaped in these parts of the society was different.

I also quickly realized that the most common imagery of womanhood and manhood depicted young or middle-aged adults. Imagery of children and of elderly adults was either uncommon or absent, depending on the medium. In ceramic figurines, elderly men and women, infants held in arms, and children appear. In carved stone monuments, even people described in accompanying texts as young children were depicted as if they were smaller-scale adults, while other people whose advanced age was recorded in the texts were represented as in the prime of life. Why would monumental art insist on showing everyone as if they were young adults? If we remember that images serve as patterns against which we measure ourselves, then this makes sense: not unlike modern fashion ads, the patrons and artists of these Classic Maya images wanted to project an ideal to which the population could compare themselves. Modern fashion ads are shaped by companies to persuade consumers to continually buy new products that promise to help them achieve an impossible look. Classic Maya monuments were patronized by Classic Maya rulers and nobles. Their interests were in persuading people that the rulers were the ideal against which everyone else should be measured.

The figures depicted in monuments offered a clear image of heterosexual adult gender performance that was simultaneously a precedent for the enactment of noble status and public formality. That sex mattered in formal public performances by the nobility was suggested by the frequency with which female images were paired with male images. Tatiana Proskouriakoff's research had originally called attention to the presence of female figures standing at ground level gazing up at the enthroned males in "ascension scenes" from Piedras Negras (see fig. 22).[18] Female figures also were juxtaposed with male figures through the creation of paired monuments that stood facing each other in many Classic Maya sites.

Following from a suggestion by the influential feminist theorist Judith Butler that gender is a kind of "incessant action," I paid as much attention to what different figures were doing as I did to the visual clues in clothing that, following Proskouriakoff, I used to recognize female and male figures. In monumental images, what I found was that most actions were common to men and women. Men and women both held the most important symbols of royal power, a bar with heads of a serpent on both ends, or an axe with a handle in the form of an image of a Maya deity. Both men and women stood on the backs of defeated warriors. Even the display of shields and weapons by male figures was echoed by the female figures (fig. 32). These actions together formed what Joyce Marcus called an "iconography of power," the kinds of actions expected of ruling factions.[19] Rather than discriminate between the sexes, these images presented both men and women as members of the ruling faction.

A few actions were depicted that were uncommon for males, sometimes shared by female figures and male servants. Noble females were depicted holding bundles wrapped in cloth, or open bowls or baskets (fig. 33). Unwrapped bundles and bowls contained objects used in ceremony and ritual. In these images, noble women paired with men assisted them in ceremonies that were

32 Classic Maya sculpture showing woman holding round shield.

33 Classic Maya sculpture showing woman holding cloth bundle.

part of political ritual. I saw these gestures as having other potential readings, linked to other visual media: figurines and pottery vessels.

Mixing media: Monuments and figurines

I originally began examining figurines and painted and carved vessels because monuments were never going to provide information about the experience of anyone except a small ruling clique. Some scholars argue that the values promoted by these small groups established the conditions of existence and the values for everyone in Classic Maya society. Like other researchers, I disagree, and consider that there can be substantial differences in the way people outside the inner elites carried out their lives, and what values they maintained. Even within the noble segment of society, I expected that there would be tensions between the values of the ruling families and those of other noble families. Within noble families, I suspected that people of different ages and social positions would have had different values as well.

Very few houses of the laborers who did most of the work in Classic Maya society have been excavated, but a variety of noble houses have been explored. Excavations in noble houses have produced many ceramic figurines and pots with figural motifs. Two things stand out when these visual representations are compared to the images on contemporary monuments. First, there is a much greater diversity overall in the kinds of human experience represented in ceramic art. Men and women of many ages, from children to the elderly, are included. The range of actions shown is considerably more varied. While the range of actions of men overlaps with those on monuments, many actions performed by women in these smaller-scale images were unknown from monuments. Instead of simply offering bowls and bundles of cloth, female figures were shown grinding corn and weaving cloth (see fig. 27). Female figures were shown holding bowls containing round balls likely to be tamales or other foods. I suggested that cloth bundles and open bowls held by noble women in scenes on monuments would have recalled for their viewers the end products of work that women were shown doing in small-scale images circulating in noble households at the same time.

Second, while many aspects of representation of adult human figures in small-scale images paralleled monumental images, women's costume commonly revealed breasts (see fig. 11), concealed in monumental sculpture by richly textured robes. Archaeologist Karen Olsen Bruhns has pointed out that the rich costumes worn by women on Classic Maya monuments have a parallel in the lavish court costumes of European queens.[20] We do not assume that the average European woman wore courtly attire, and similarly the robes worn by noble women were more than the typical costume of their sex: they were expressions of performance of a public role limited to women of a specific social status. Some of the robes women wore on monuments were part of the costume of figures named as males in texts on monuments, evidence for "cross-dressing" that remains a subject of debate in Maya studies.[21]

Based on all these observations, it seemed to me that monuments, far from being concerned to emphasize gender difference, presented men and women together as part of a ruling group with common interests and values. Where figurines and pots displayed a wide range of bodily differences, including those of age and sex, monuments depicted idealized young adults, the image of ageless power projected by the nobility. Where figurines and pots suggested a wide range of activities carried out by men and women, including tasks distinctive of each, monuments presented joint performance of ritual actions.

Looking at bodies

The way women's robes were carved on monuments was curiously unrelated to the contours of the bodies they covered. The same monuments lovingly detailed the arms, torso, and legs of noble men. While both men and women were presented in idealized youth, their bodies made beautiful by rich jewelry and elaborate clothing, I began to think that I needed to examine more closely how Classic Maya visual imagery portrayed bodily experience itself.

Whether in monuments or the multi-figure compositions painted or carved on pottery vessels (fig. 34), the young, active male body was the object of the gaze of both older males and adult women.[22] On painted pottery depicting court scenes, older seated males glanced toward groups of warriors, athletes, and dancers. On monuments, women gazed upward at seated or standing men. The profusion of male images in Maya visual media provided ample evidence of the idealization of young, active male bodies as objects of contemplation by both men and women. I suggested that in this sector of Classic Maya society, the young male exemplified beauty, and admiration of male youths by both men and women was modeled as normal.

If the beauty of young males was admired in Maya society, could this suggest that such admiration led to same-sex relationships between males? This is a controversial argument, one not easily accepted, given the basic homophobia of modern archaeology. When heterosexual activity is considered the norm, same-sex relationships can be recognized only as abnormal or transgressive, not as accepted or idealized. Contemporary archaeologists share wider cultural orientations that merge a fascination with sex with a tendency to see sex as private and potentially a source of public shame. Archaeology can provide powerful reminders that this is a modern attitude, one with a history that is very well known but whose effects on our reading of clues to the past needs to be more clearly acknowledged.

Space and sex

Sex was not always as closely policed or separated into a sphere of privacy in past societies. In her studies of the houses of New Kingdom Egyptian laborers working on royal tombs at Deir el Medina, archaeologist Lynn Meskell drew attention to the prominence of sexual imagery in the most public reception rooms.[23] Similar observations could be made about the interior decoration of Classical Greek and Roman houses. Nor is less privacy surrounding sex simply part of a European tradition. Archaeologist Barbara Voss, writing about the

colonization of native Californian societies, noted that the Spanish missionaries were intent on segregating women and men at night in sleeping quarters, to avoid sexual activity between them. Yet in these native Californian societies sex actually took place outside, away from houses.[24]

My initial exploration of the way all-male groups of youths were depicted as beautiful subjects in Classic Maya art led me to ask whether there was evidence for accepted practices of same-sex sociability that might have included sexuality.[25] Sixteenth-century texts describing descendants of the Classic Maya described young men as moving into common houses together, where they developed their skills at athletic contests and dances. Spanish sources accused the residents of such young men's houses of sexual crimes against young women, while asserting that sexual relations between males were not practiced. At the same time, contemporary dictionaries included entries for words describing male-male sex acts, casting some doubt on the categorical claim that no same-sex activity was practiced among the Yucatec Maya. Manuscripts written in the Yucatec Maya language in the centuries following the Spanish invasion contain many mentions of male-male sexual activity ascribed to political enemies. Because Spanish missionaries had branded such activity as sinful, we cannot assume Maya informants were open and complete in reporting who participated in same-sex encounters. Nor can these later sources be used on their own as clues to practices centuries earlier.

Many Late Classic Maya sites contained buildings that I identified as possibly the locations of young men's houses like those described in the sixteenth century. Often, these buildings are similar to contemporary residential compounds, but they may lack evidence for some domestic activities, such as cooking. They may be larger, able to accommodate more residents than other contemporary houses. Examples at sites including Chichén Itzá and Uxmal were ornamented with large-scale

34 Court scene on Classic Maya polychrome pot.

phallic sculptures. Buildings of this kind could be located close to ballgame courts. Some have scenes of dancing and athletic ball-playing carved on them, reminding us of the close association between young men and public displays of prowess in dances and games seen in Classic Maya art and sixteenth-century texts.

Actual scenes of sexual activity of any kind are extremely rare in Classic Maya sites, and none are yet known in residential contexts. Naj Tunich cave has produced several images of sexual acts. Here, art historian Andrea Stone has identified scenes of male masturbation in close proximity to an image of two nude standing figures shown in profile, locked in an embrace. One figure has an erect penis, and the other was originally interpreted as his female consort. Subsequently, Stone called attention to details of the second figure more likely to be seen on a Classic Maya male, suggesting the embracing pair were two males.[26]

The proposal that there were special places in some Classic Maya cities where young men socialized together, and perhaps resided, is fairly uncontroversial. Taking the next step and suggesting that the young men in these sites experienced same-sex desire and acted on it, however, has literally created a backlash among some scholars. One of the interesting aspects of this backlash has been the clear assumption that same-sex desire and practice would be incompatible with the social value placed on male-female sex by social groups like those of the Postclassic Maya and Mexica, among whom reproduction of the social group was represented as a duty to family and state. The heteronormative perspective demands that people have one naturally given sexual orientation, and allows for same-sex desire only if it is an exception that literally proves the rule. Longing gazes focused on young male bodies, whether from men or women, are pervasive in Classic Maya visual culture, which presents young male bodies as objects of desire while simultaneously recognizing male-female parents and their children as important subjects.

How a regime of bodily precedents for the sexuality of men and women, like Classic Maya images, was related to sexual lives and understandings of reproduction should be an open topic for research. The assumption that male-female sex was the dominant norm in ancient societies, incompatible with other forms of sexual experience, supplies a pre-existing answer before the question of other forms of sexual activity has been asked.

Sexual reproduction beyond the heterosexual couple

Along the arid northern coast of Peru, a series of rivers create the only locations for agricultural societies to thrive. In some of these river valleys, archaeologists have recently excavated lavish tombs of the Moche, a society known for pottery with explicit depiction of sex acts. In these tombs, a single central person, biologically male, was laid to rest wearing costumes incorporating ornaments of precious metals. Other males and females were placed in other parts of the burial mound, often also dressed in expensive costumes. Included with the principal and secondary burials were large numbers of vessels modeled and painted in the Moche style. Based on study of vessels in museum collections, art historians and archaeologists recognize many of the people in these recently documented burials as wearing costumes shown in scenes on the vases. The range of ceremonies depicted is great, and includes scenes interpreted as ritual battles and human sacrifices, and others identified as burial rituals.[27]

Archaeologists and art historians have emphasized the degree to which the sexual acts shown on some Moche pots depart from the expectations of hetero-normativity. Oral and anal sex are common, leading scholars to suggest that Moche sexuality as portrayed in this medium was centered on the satisfaction of the male to the exclusion of the sexuality of the female. Researchers routinely describe the sex depicted as "non-reproductive." The terms of debate have thus been drawn in terms of heteronormative understandings of sexuality, in which the introduction of the male penis in the female vagina for the purpose of insemination is normal, and other actions are deviant.[28]

Anthropologist Mary Weismantel approaches these same objects from a very different perspective, informed by critiques of heteronormativity and knowledge gained from her work as an ethnographer studying kinship and the reproduction of families in the Ecuadorian Andes.[29] She begins by noting that we cannot assume that ancient Moche people had the same understanding of sexual reproduction as twentieth-century Europeans and North Americans. So we cannot label any of the sex acts depicted as non-reproductive simply because our model of sexual reproduction does not require them. Weismantel notes that ethnographers have described many theories of sexual reproduction in which the circulation of substances necessary for the successful development of infants involves actions other than coitus. What is seen as reproductive depends in part on how people think babies take form. The actions required may involve people other than the two recognized as father and mother in heteronormative models of sex.

Documents recorded in the language of the Mexica of Central Mexico in the sixteenth century using the European alphabet provide an illustration. Young women were understood to become pregnant partly through the efforts of specific supernatural beings. Sexual intercourse was not effective without the actions of these beings. Once pregnant, the development of the infant required sweat baths carried out in the house compound, under the direction of midwives. Without the efforts of the gods and the women who assisted in the sweat bath, the infant might be born without internal vital force, or could be hollow inside and die.[30] We do not have full descriptions of the understanding of sexual reproduction current in Mexica society, but even the fragments preserved in sixteenth-century texts suggest theories of reproduction in which children were products of a network of living people and supernatural beings much wider than the male-female couple contemporary scholars might credit as parents.

Weismantel suggests that Moche people connected the sexual acts depicted on their pots with the transmission of ancestral substances over generations, from the dead through the living. She notes the juxtaposition of sex acts with skeletal figures and funeral rites, jarring to contemporary archaeologists, and suggests the sexual acts depicted linked not just the two bodies involved but also their deceased ancestors. She challenges the assertion that anal and oral sex were not understood as contributing to the formation of infant bodies, perhaps through models, different from those of modern America and Europe, of circulation of bodily substances from one body to the other. Noting the repeated presence of nursing children in Moche sex scenes (fig. 35), Weismantel suggests that the Moche sex pots are eminently social: not media celebrating adult male sexual experience, but rather, connections much broader than imagined under the heteronormative model, between ancestors and children, mediated by adult sexuality.

Sex beyond reproduction

According to documents created in the sixteenth century, celibacy was one of the normal options in the lives of Mexica, a future to which children were dedicated while still very young.[31] Children destined for life in temple service were raised within their households of birth until they were young teens. In a very real sense, Mexica households thus contained children of many different sexes: boys and girls destined for sexual activity in adulthood, and children who would remain celibate.

Heteronormativity leads to resistance to suggestions of same-sex relations in the past, and to universalizing one model of sexual reproduction. It also can cause us to ignore sexual lives that stand outside the reproductive grid. Archaeologists have produced rich accounts of sexual lives that include both celibacy and sex work. These contribute significant examples of how people's experiences developed in relation to social expectations about sexuality in the past.

After the defeat of the Mexica state by the Spanish, descriptions of the training of children were created for the new authorities. In these, boys were

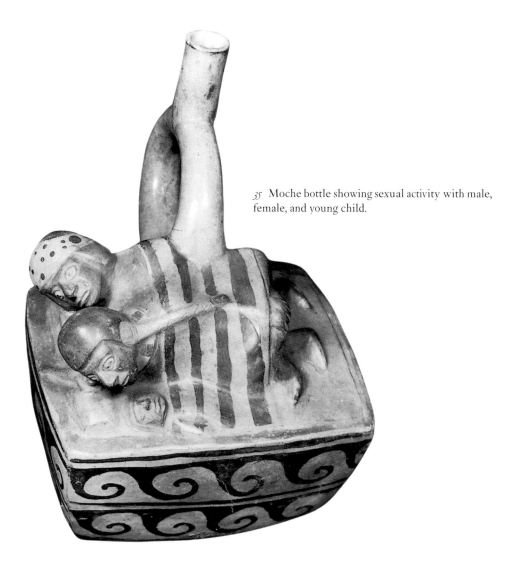

35 Moche bottle showing sexual activity with male, female, and young child.

shown being trained by fathers in tasks they might carry out in adulthood, such as collecting wood and fishing, and girls being taught by their mothers to spin, weave and carry out other household tasks (see fig. 31). Such accounts leave out children destined for temple service. Were they trained in the same fashion, or subject to another form of education? We know that both boys and girls in temple service occupied themselves sweeping the precincts. Anthropologist Louise Burkhart demonstrates that for adult women, sweeping the home compound was a ritual action that paralleled and supported the participation of men of the house in battle. Were boys destined for temple service trained in their birth households in this cross-sex task?[32] Geoffrey and Sharisse McCafferty have explored how adult women in temple service were able to act in many of the same ways as adult men. Did their predestination for life in temples lead to different opportunities as young girls?[33]

While documents prepared for Spanish consumption are silent about the inculcation of children in sexual life, it is likely that this was also part of what young children learned, either directly or indirectly, during childhood. Celibate children must have been subject to different expectations and instruction by older adults in their households of birth. The knowledge that some of the children in Mexica households were already destined for lives as celibate adults means that our interpretations of the material traces of those households have to involve more than the dichotomous, heterosexual, reproductive models on which we have largely depended. Houses were sites where children learned many ways to experience sexuality. Temple compounds in Mexica cities were locations where children turned adults perfected their performances of this form of sexual life.

Celibacy in place

Celibate adults often occupy spatial precincts of their own. Medieval England is one example of a place and time where the lives of sexually abstinent people shaped the traces that archaeologists today can explore. Archaeologist Roberta Gilchrist examines how the denial of physical sensuality, and the enclosure of religious women in nunneries, promoted an interiorized experience of sexuality through the orientation of desire toward Christ.[34] Gilchrist uses texts describing medieval beliefs about the nature of women and expectations of religious men and women to show that religious women were expected to maintain seclusion from the outside world, while remaining incorporated in a community of women.

Churches always required the presence of male priests, and were often shared with male religious communities or the lay parish. So the segregation of women religious is visible in the plans of churches. These sometimes include chambers for women religious who chose a life of absolute seclusion.

Archaeological excavations of women's religious institutions documented more primitive levels of sanitation, more trash, and poorer food than contemporary institutions of male religious. Gilchrist suggests this needs to be seen in relation to the textual emphasis on women religious needing to discipline their bodies. The outcome of such practices would be the realization of internal communion with God. Gilchrist suggests that internal communion of nuns with Christ was the subject of the visual images that are preserved in women's religious institutions of the time. Drawing on accounts of women's visions, Gilchrist argues that while male authorities saw the institutionalization of female religious as a denial of bodily sexuality, their own experience was of themselves as sexual beings turned inward.

Among all the traces of the lives of men and women in the past, architecture is a particularly valuable source of evidence for archaeologists simply because buildings are very durable, always found in their original location and even when in ruins, preserve their plan. Buildings were not just places where people carried out their daily lives. Just as importantly, buildings coordinated the experiences of individual people and induced differences between them. Seclusion from the broader community, segregation of certain people in some areas, and exclusion from others, all change the nature, frequency, and intimacy of experiences of other people. Because other people are models for the performance of gender (as much as images of people, or even more), changes in the frequency and intimacy of contact with others changes what we take as our models for action. In cloistered religious communities composed only of women, like those investigated by Gilchrist, the patterns for gender performance and the authorities approving or disapproving of the gendered actions of others were different than in the mixed-sex communities outside the walls of the enclosure.

The place of sex in the recent past

In cities across the United States in the nineteenth and early twentieth centuries, communities of women lived together outside the normative regime of heterosexual experience. Like medieval nuns, the buildings they occupied provide archaeologists today with clues to the ways that their distinctive sexual lives altered their everyday experiences. These women were sex-workers living in brothels, which have been uncovered as projects of urban renewal have taken place in areas of cities where cultural practices disapproved of by central authorities but tacitly tolerated were once allowed to flourish.[35]

Brothel sites are from one perspective no different than any other site of residence. In them, archaeologists find material traces of everyday life, of food preparation and consumption, of expressive activities, of birth, illness, and death. But we know that the participants in sexual activities at these places were bound by commercial transactions, not just by affective bonds. The temptation to present these sites simply as places where sexual norms were transgressed is strong. In fact, they help us understand the degree to which practices seen in other households represent widely shared values. Archaeological studies provide a sense of what life was like in these establishments in comparison to the lives lived by people in the same areas not employed in sex work.

The residents of a late nineteenth-century brothel in central Washington, DC, bought and consumed luxury foods and drink, and luxurious tablewares, to a much greater degree than other contemporary households.[36] A rich deposit of garbage was found buried in the lot next to this house, located only steps from the US Capitol building. This trash was compared to samples of garbage from other late nineteenth-century house lots throughout Washington.

The serving wares discarded by the residents and customers at this brothel included the most current pottery, ironstone and porcelain, with elegant decoration. The quantity of serving dishes recovered is consistent with a much higher number of people being served food than in neighboring households. The food served was also distinctive: French champagne, beef, pork, and mutton, meats among the most expensive available, as well as wild birds, turtles, fish, fruits, berries, and vegetables, and costly imported coconuts and brazil nuts were all represented by discarded bones, seeds, and containers. Through their participation in sex work, the women who lived here effectively became part of a large household with a high standard of living that would otherwise likely not have been available to them.

A second late nineteenth-century brothel, this one located in Los Angeles, California, had a similar diversity of serving wares of good quality and evidence of food and drink.[37] Preserved below the asphalt surface of a parking lot, archaeologists found traces of house foundations, trash pits, wells, and backyard privies filled in after they fell out of use.

At the Los Angeles site, researchers documented some of the special challenges of life in the sex trade. Drugs to prevent conception, to cure venereal disease, painkillers and beauty creams were more abundant than in neighboring houses whose residents were not engaged in prostitution. Traces of efforts sex-workers made to control their chances of getting pregnant, as well as the remains of newborn and unborn infants, are known at other brothel sites as well. While many houses of prostitution have produced fine serving wares and varied and expensive foods, in some it is equally clear that in everyday practice, the women working at the brothels did not enjoy the use of fancy pottery or access to exceptional foods, which instead were part of setting the scene for visiting patrons.[38]

For the women who worked in them, brothels may have been one of the few avenues to earn enough money to live. Their material traces represent households composed largely of working women whose experiences of sexuality separated them from other women in the cities where they lived. The sense of self of the occupants of these places would have been different from that normally expected for their sex and class, even though the things through which they practiced their gendered performances were mainly shared with other women living in more conventional households. The traces in brothel sites of their efforts to manage their vulnerability to pregnancy and sexually transmitted diseases should remind us that similar challenges must have been being managed by women and men in other times and places. Taking men's and women's lives as sexual beings seriously raises a whole new set of research questions for contemporary archaeology. These questions require archaeologists to consider the experiences of sex of their subjects in the past and preclude any approach in which gender and sex are treated separately, one as a merely categorical identity and the other as a biological reality.

A future for sex in the past

Archaeology has come a long way from a search for women in the past. Understanding sex and gender requires us to avoid initial categorizations or we will always find what such categorizations assume is there. In return, we gain a renewed appreciation for the particulars of history, and for the way that individual lives derive their meaning from their connection to enduring histories and values projected in art and material culture. Archaeology of sex and gender now encompasses multiple forms of masculinity as much as it does femininity. It explores sexual relations that diverge radically from contemporary norms, and engages with cultures whose ideas about sexuality and reproduction challenge what we take for granted today. Sexual difference is still a real subject of study, but now, we understand that we need to question whether the differences we see result from aspects of personhood distinct from sex or gender. The resources available for this investigation include both the physical traces of lived lives in the bones left behind by the dead, images of the living, and the remains of the houses, temples, and possessions used everyday and on special occasions. Everything in an archaeological site has the potential to speak to questions of sex and gender.

Roberta Gilchrist, drawing on the work of philosopher Elizabeth Grosz, insists that study of sex must take into account how social experiences of gender go beyond a superficial "inscription" of bodily appearance and action to a deeper reflection on how experience affects people's sense of themselves. Grosz suggests that people's experience forms their psychological understanding of themselves. Her own preferred image for the kinds of analyses gender studies should promote is a Möbius strip: a single ribbon of paper, given a half-twist and taped together so that inside and outside are joined in a continuous loop. In a Möbius strip there are not two sides, a superficial exterior and a more real interior, but only one. Experience is not more superficial than identity; identity is not deeper than appearance; appearance, experience, and a continually shifting sense of self flow together. Like other theorists who have proved important to contemporary archaeologies of gender, Grosz rejects the sex/gender binary because it treats one term as more fundamental and the other as more superficial, one as enduring and the other as fleeting.[39]

The goal of archaeologies of sex and gender is no longer simply a corrective search for women's presence in the past, or the explication of the historical development of domination of men over women. Where once archaeology was a source of examples of exceptional situations of female power in the past, today, archaeologists critique overly simple interpretations of their data as evidence of matriarchy, Amazons, and queens. Much of the explicitly feminist archaeological work that has been accomplished in recent decades through such specialties as household archaeology has taken the lives of ordinary people as a focus, describing women and men in what seem at first glance to be traditional divisions of labor and authority. What, then, does archaeological gender analysis add to contemporary women's and gender studies?

5

Living as men and women

The evidence with which archaeologists work – remains of a meal, figurines, fragments of a bowl – are not simply traces of *how* people lived their lives in the past, but actually things that transformed how people lived their lives. The past embraces more different ways of human life than exist in the contemporary world, or even that segment of past experience represented in written documents. Archaeological analyses offer the potential for discovering ways of human life in which experiences of sex were different from any we would otherwise imagine. The goal of archaeologies of sex and gender is to open up a whole new way of looking at the lived experiences of people in the past, especially those experiences that varied because of differences in sex and sexuality. As a materialist discipline, dependent on teasing out information from even the most modest material traces of people in the past, archaeology has a particular ability to show how people's lives are bound up in materiality, and how the world of things at different times and places actively shaped distinctive experiences.

Contemporary women's and gender studies recognize that while women have repeatedly been disadvantaged as a class in respect to men, people of different class, race, ethnicity, age, and reproductive histories have had unique advantages and disadvantages that cannot be collapsed into a single categorical topic of woman's or man's experience. The archaeology of being male and female, of being persons with desires and life experiences dependent on sexuality that are varied along lines of class, ethnicity, and race, is at the forefront of studies of gender in the past being conducted by archaeologists today. Contemporary archaeologies of gender replace the simple stereotypes we once offered with richer accounts of people in the past that ultimately contribute better weapons in the battle to argue that nature is not destiny and that inequities based on gender are not historically inevitable.

Making a meaningful life: The archaeology of an African-American midwife

Historical archaeologists George Shorter and Laurie Wilkie, working in a park in Mobile, Alabama that was being landscaped in 1994, excavated two buried deposits that related to a late nineteenth- to early twentieth-century house site. While previous work on the park had stripped away anything that would have remained of the ground surface from this early period, these two buried deposits turned out to have a wealth of information from two moments in the life of an African-American family, of Marshall and Lucretia Perryman and their children. Their life at this site began around 1869, and Lucretia's children continued to control the land for about ten years after her death in 1917. The first preserved collection of trash was buried in a shallow pit dated to around 1885, the second in an abandoned well filled in around 1911. The trash discarded in 1885 consisted of around 100 fragments of glass bottles and 150 pieces from pottery vessels, representing parts of around 55 individual objects used and discarded by the family. The well produced a larger and more diverse sample of trash, including pieces of almost 70 pottery vessels, more than 50 distinct glass serving vessels, over 80 different glass bottles, and a variety of other objects, both decorative and functional, from porcelain figurines to almost 300 fragments of bones from cuts of meat consumed by the residents. From these two excavated assemblages, archaeologist Laurie Wilkie built up a picture of daily life at the Perryman house.[1]

Lucretia Perryman, a free woman who began her life in slavery, was recorded as working as a midwife in documents beginning in 1889, continuing in practice until at least 1907. Wilkie brought to her research an interest in the experiences of people of different sexes, races, and social status groups. Her analyses culminated in a rich explication of the way that a midwife like Perryman affected her community. Her study is a model of how self-conscious interests in gendered experience can transform archaeological interpretation.

Wilkie identifies many of the discarded containers of commercial products, such as vaseline, cologne, and cod liver oil, not simply as generally available commodities used by the household, but as products employed by midwives in their practice. Starting with the material remains, Wilkie draws on historic sources to explore how these things were used. Among the materials she encountered were many that were used in nineteenth-century practices intended to control sexuality, not just practices related to pregnancy and childbirth. Wilkie suggests that Perryman occupied a critical role in the regulation of sexuality in her community, using tools such as a douche syringe and the patent medicines and pharmaceuticals for which over 120 discarded bottles were found in the old well as materials for birth control.

Exploring other artifacts that would have been used or displayed in the household, Wilkie is able to draw out connections with ideals of mothering in late nineteenth-century America, ideals to which Perryman subscribed strongly enough to expend money on purchases.[2] Fragments of porcelain figurines discarded in the well would once have decorated the interior of the house, seen by visiting clients and neighbors. Wilkie teases out the values of late-Victorian society that made these mass-produced figurines popular, and shows how the ones selected by the Perrymans would have had particular relevance to a midwife. A pair of cherubs, one playing a musical instrument, the other with a hand to its ear, listening to the song, exemplified the ideal childhood body, with "soft, round cheeks, full pouty lips, and gently curly hair" and "nicely formed limbs and full bellies." A matchbox from the well was decorated with a classical image, a woman feeding an eagle, likely a reference to the Greek myth of Zeus and Semele, the mother of Dionysus, whose rescue from his mother's dying body provides a precedent for birth by cesarean section. Pieces of dolls, including a large "Floradora" doll and a small "Frozen Charlotte," may seem incidental to the work of a midwife. But Wilkie assembles documents including mothering manuals, ads, and editorials from the national leaders of the African-American community, that show that toys had recognized roles to play in shaping ideals of family life.

From the relatively modest assemblage of trash discarded at this site, Wilkie develops a rich picture of the life of Lucretia Perryman, who was born in slavery, a condition in which she would not have completely controlled her own reproduction or the fates of her children, and ended her life providing moral guidance and medical assistance to new mothers. What would have been different about this study if it had been conducted before archaeologists began to consider questions of sex and gender?

How thinking about sex changes archaeology

The description of the contents of the well would probably have been generically interpreted as evidence of consumption of items bought by a typical household, perhaps recognized as an example of generalized African-American life or the life of the working poor. In that generic picture, women would have been assumed to be playing the part of maintaining the domestic front while men, employed outside the house, were engaged in the primary wage-earning. Women in the household would have been understood as relatively passive compared to men. Specific sexual experience would never even have been raised, as households were treated as units composed of adults and children with no consideration of how children came to exist, or how they learned to understand their own roles as adults over time.

If Wilkie's studies had taken place in the first rush of archaeologies of gender, she might have looked at the materials recovered for evidence of the activities of men and women. Some items would have been attributed to one sex or the other, and the presence of both sexes – already built into the model – would presumably have been confirmed. Depending on her approach to the question of male and female roles, she might have searched the historical records for evidence that women were economically disadvantaged, or lacked the power to legally control their own lives.

Because the study actually was informed by richer approaches of gender studies, especially the perspectives of African-American scholars exploring women's lives, what Wilkie did is quite different. Knowing that one of the members of the Perryman house had been a midwife allowed her to think through the way mothering was experienced by women at the time and place, including the values of family that developed among the formerly enslaved after emancipation. She thus recognized that in this time and place, a woman whose role was quite traditional, and who operated out of the home site, could be an influential community figure.

Beyond the reinterpretations of consumer commodities that ensued, Wilkie re-imagined the lives of the Perrymans and their neighbors. She offers a picture of Lucretia Perryman self-consciously shaping motherhood in the African-

American community along the lines of late nineteenth-century ideals of domesticity. She takes us into the Perryman's family as it grew and acquired land through the work of Lucretia's husband, who overcame the potential limitations of never learning to read by calling on the white employer he identified in his will as his friend to act as his agent and trustee. She shows how Lucretia's choice of work after Marshall's death allowed her to stay out of personal service, maintaining a degree of autonomy prized in the post-Civil War African-American community. She lets us see the children and grandchildren of this couple growing up, marrying, gaining the formal education their parents had been denied, returning to the home property when the death of a spouse or an illness required.

Living a good life

In the Upper Mantaro Valley of Peru, conquest by the Inka state in the fifteenth century transformed many aspects of everyday life. The new empire demanded labor from men, and in return, workers on state projects were provided foods made from maize. Because maize differs from other plants in the way carbon is incorporated in tissues, archaeologist Christine Hastorf was able to measure the levels of maize consumed by men and women before and after the Inka conquest (see fig. 16). She showed that men consumed maize in greater quantities than the women left behind in the towns. The biological differences Hastorf documented between men and women are historically specific patterns, the result of imperial labor organization, not universal or innate life courses determined by sex.[3] Studies like this use methods from the chemical and physical sciences to understand the way that people of different sexes lived, aged, and died.

Bioarchaeologists can detect traces left in the human skeleton of differences between people in nutrition, in disease, and in habitual work. Most of these studies begin by assuming that males and females would always show categorical differences.[4] Some studies find such differences, while others discover patterns in which factors such as age, class, or lifestyle are more significant.

In studies of access to different dietary resources among the Classic Maya, bioarchaeologist Christine White found more consistent differences between members of the ruling group and those they ruled than between men and women. Diets varied greatly between sites, and distinctions between men and women varied over time. The most strongly marked differences between male and female life experiences were found in the noble populations, where men ate more maize, more meat (including marine fish), and in particular, more meat from deer and dogs whose own diets, heavy in maize, suggest they were raised for use on special occasions. In limited samples of the population of laborers, men and women had diets that were virtually the same. Much of the variability noted in the noble groups may have resulted from men being more likely to consume distinctive food on ritual occasions.[5]

Taking similar osteobiographical approaches and looking at variation over time, researchers throughout the world have demonstrated variability in whether, when, and how much the nutrition, health, and work of men and women differed. Bioarchaeologists working at some sites in the southeastern United States found that over time, increasing centralization and intensification of maize farming were accompanied by distinct traces of repetitive labor, women's bodies reflecting grain grinding and men's the use of bows and arrows.[6] Other bioarchaeologists identified potential evidence of differences in suffering from violence in higher incidences of fractures in the lower arm bones among women in some archaeological sites, as a result of lifting the arm to ward off a blow, traces of the periodic experience of warfare.[7]

Sex, age, and health

Work by bioarchaeologist Sabrina Agarwal on historic British populations directly challenges one of the most widely accepted contemporary assumptions about sexual lives: that with age, women are uniquely subject to bone fragility and bone fracture, the injuries we label osteoporosis.[8] Agarwal studies the patterns of bone growth and fractures, and carefully distinguishes the traces of fractures caused by bone loss with aging. Such bone loss following age-related changes in estrogen levels today is treated as an almost unavoidable part of women's experience. What Agarwal found in comparisons of Roman London, the medieval village of Wharram Percy in Yorkshire, and AD 1770 to 1850 working-class London, is something quite different. Women in all three times and places did not show bone loss between middle and old age, despite our modern expectations. Nor was there simply a single, easy to interpret pattern of increasing fragility of bone over time. Agarwal identifies differences in work, patterns of childbirth, and breast-feeding practices as the root causes of men's and women's experiences of bone loss in aging.

In Roman London, women suffered their most marked bone loss during the transition from young adult to middle age. This pattern held for all three populations that Agarwal studied, vividly contrasting with the modern expectation that women's bone health will decline with their entry into old age. Why the difference? Agarwal suggests that younger and middle-aged women who had recently given birth in these three populations were responsible for the pattern of bone loss between youth and middle age, since pregnancy and breast-feeding produce temporary bone loss. By the time women were entering old age at these sites, their bodies had recovered from these stresses of child-rearing, and these women may actually have been partly protected from bone loss with old age by their histories of reproduction and nursing. In other words, bone loss with aging, while biologically shaped, was not an automatic experience of all women in the past, nor need it be today.

Agarwal actually found no significant differences in bone loss with old age between men and women in any of her three samples. Men were actually more likely than women to have bone loss at the onset of old age in Roman London and in late pre-industrial London. This is the kind of bone loss today assumed to be specifically the lot of women. Men in these populations did not have the advantages conferred on women by childbirth and nursing.

But at rural Wharram Percy, even this apparent sex-based variation did not occur. Neither women nor men showed the kind of bone loss with old age expected in modern populations. The men of Wharram Percy were subject to more bone loss with the transition from youth to middle age than were the women of this village. Agarwal suggests that possibly the histories of childbirth – the high number of babies each woman had and breast-feeding for long periods – by women of Wharram Percy provided them with an even greater advantage in a place where nutrition for both men and women was poor, and where life was marked by intensive physical activity that could easily cause brittle bones to break.

The most striking thing about the evidence for bone loss among both men and women at Wharram Percy is the low prevalence in both sexes of the kinds of fractures that can be attributed to changing levels of sex hormones with age. Life in rural villages like these, when compared to life in a city such as London from its earliest history to the present, was marked by heavy burdens of physical labor. The exercise undertaken in everyday life by the villagers of Wharram Percy helped keep their bones stronger. London residents from the eighteenth and nineteenth centuries, both men and women, were more like modern city-dwellers, working at jobs that did not keep up their bone strength as they aged.

Agarwal notes that in both Wharram Percy and later London, childbirth was likely not delayed, as it is often today. Women who gave birth were much more likely to breast-feed. These activities contributed to remodeling of bone in the bodies of women who gave birth, especially if they prolonged breast-feeding. The lives of men and women in rural Wharram Percy were athletic enough overall that this sex-based difference did not emerge as the basis for significant differences in the experiences of men and women in old age. But in London, where both men and women lived lives with less physical activity, women who gave birth and breast-fed experienced less bone loss and bone fracture than their equally sedentary male counterparts. While women in later London were still breast-feeding, historic sources suggest that weaning was earlier and thus the positive effects of this practice on bone would have been weaker than at medieval Wharram Percy. Owing to larger normal family size and breast-feeding in all these historic populations, most women would have been less exposed to estrogen during their lives than women today.

These observed patterns challenge modern assumptions, and also illustrate the importance of particular historic conditions in the outcome of what many people today consider an inherent sex-based aspect of health in aging. Only in the most recent urban population studied was there a clear difference by sex in the experience of bone loss. In all three periods, women's bone loss happened earlier than the transition to old age that we associate today with the risk of osteoporosis. Agarwal explains these apparently un-natural results as reflecting factors that we ignore in thinking about osteoporosis in modern populations.

Agarwal's research project began, as do almost all bioarchaeological analyses, by dividing the population between adult males, adult females, and children too young to be assigned to male or female categories. But her actual analysis is not a simple exploration of how men and women differed, or of presumed advantages men had over women. Instead, she adopts a perspective that presumes each person had a distinct life course, in which a variety of biological and experiential features led to distinctive life histories. As called for by feminist philosophers from Elizabeth Grosz to Judith Butler, this is an analysis that takes the materiality of the body seriously, without treating it as separate from cultural life.

Lives with histories

The place today known as Deir el Medina was once a thriving village where, between 1500 and 1100 BC, generations of workers building the tombs of Egyptian pharaohs, nobles, and functionaries lived. Here, the workman Nebamun and his wife lived in a house whose outer room was decorated by a painting of a nude female musician, a sexualized image typical of such spaces, likely used in part for everyday work but also for household rituals related to the lives of adult women. Like other men of the town, Nebamun would have used the second room in the house both to receive visitors, and as a site for rituals directed at his ancestors. Archaeologist Lynn Meskell demonstrates that sexual difference mattered at Deir el Medina, but it was not the single difference that determined the course of people's lives. The wife of a wealthy man, like Merit, the spouse of the royal architect Kha, could expect very unequal treatment when buried in her husband's tomb, receiving only a fraction of the goods dedicated to him, in part because of the greater importance men assumed as ancestors for the male heirs who buried them. But among less wealthy families, a woman might find her life course determined more by age or marital status. Like another woman named Nub, whose life is recorded in texts from the site, she might end her life buried in a more modest tomb of her own, surrounded by her personal belongings, buried carefully by her adult children, who would otherwise risk being disinherited, the fate of the children of another woman, Naunakhte, for whom we have historical records.[9]

Archaeological studies like these, even when they draw on historical documents, always give priority to the materiality of traces of past human action. It is not simply a given that African-American midwives would use consumer goods in a particular way. The practices of the villagers of Wharram Percy are more in evidence through the remains of their village than through the limited contemporary documentary record. While the documents from Deir el Medina name specific people, the particularities of their lives are found in the material remains of their houses and tombs.

Nonetheless, even within archaeology, studies that draw on historical documents are often treated as exceptional. Archaeologists without such resources are not expected to be able to provide similarly rich accounts of gendered lives. Rather than being due to the data archaeologists have, the important thing is whether difference is understood to be more variable, dynamic, and active from the beginning of analysis. My final example of contemporary archaeology of gender comes from a social setting where no contemporary documents written in any decipherable language exist: the Classic period societies of Caribbean coastal Honduras (ca. AD 500–1000).

If we want to conduct research specifically to understand the gendered life experiences of people in this time and place, how should we go about it? Under the approach that seeks "signatures" of sex/gender, we would first construct a model of activities we think would distinguish one sex from another.

As originally practiced, and still current today, this normally means defining some things that women do that men do not do. In normative archaeology, all activity is attributed to men unless there is an exceptional reason to think women were responsible for the actions involved. Because northern Honduras is part of a broader sphere of interlocked societies stretching from Mexico to northern Central America, the kinds of activities assumed to be those distinguishing women from men include maize grinding, food preparation, and textile production. So from the "archaeological signature" approach we might look at the distributions of grinding tools and tools of textile production to identify where women were at work. Contemporary archaeologies of sex and gender are less concerned with answering that question than with understanding how men and women lived their lives, and the values that were given to different lives at particular historical times and places. This profoundly changes what at first glance may seem like the same kind of analyses.

Crafting lives that matter

Unlike in Classic Maya sites of neighboring regions, there is very little evidence before AD 1000 of spinning or weaving in Caribbean coastal Honduras. There is more evidence for production of sheets of pressed fiber from the bark of certain trees (bark cloth or bark paper), using distinctive stone beaters. These provided archaeologist Christopher Fung one of the clues to tracing women's valued labor at a small village site in the Oloman river valley.[10] Fung's analysis did not stop at identifying the mere presence of women in households with bark beaters and grinding stones, a second material trace of women's labor that he investigated. Based on differences in the frequency of these tools in trash from different buildings, he suggested that in some households, women's work was more intensive. In houses with more evidence of grinding and bark cloth production, women's labor would have been more significant as a means for specific households to build prestige in the village as hosts for social events.

Fung's research does not treat all women in these households as the same. Rather, he assumes from the outset that differences in age and position in the family would have placed some younger people in the position of working under the direction and for the primary benefit of those older than them. The households whose discarded trash, house platforms, and yards he excavated had different levels of interest in the pursuit of social distinction. The women in these households were not interchangeable, and may have shared more with men of the same relative age and family position than with each other. In this small cross-section of one rural village, some young women would have worked harder than others the same age, not because they were women, but because their families were seeking status and they were not in positions of authority. Older women in some households would have shared the ambitions of men of their age and family, to make a distinctive show on the occasion other people visited the site when ball games were held in the adjacent ballcourt. Some such women might have privately or even publicly claimed greater credit for the house gaining stature, because of their roles in organizing feasts, dances, and rituals.

Even in this small rural village, we can tell that people cared about how they were perceived. They invested effort and energy in making human images, and the technology they used allowed participation in crafting images by people without requiring great levels of skill. Fragments of many human figurines made with molds were recovered with the other discarded materials around these houses. They are the traces of events in which images of men, women, and children were displayed, and likely talked about. The diversity of these human images provides another way to examine gendered experiences in northern Honduras during the late Classic period.

In contemporary villages throughout the lower Ulúa river valley, downstream from the Oloman house sites, mold-made figurines were produced in great numbers and a variety of sizes. Because they were made using molds, also made of fired clay, it was possible for archaeologist Jeanne Lopiparo to identify sites where figurines were being made.[11] In four villages located within a few miles of each other, she excavated molds and mold-made figures, most broken and discarded, and a few, including some very large examples, carefully placed in construction fill during the remodeling of houses. In households at two of these sites, she was able to identify where the figurines were fired.

Lopiparo noted a paradoxical fact: while the use of molds has commonly been taken by archaeologists as a way to accommodate mass production for wholesale distribution in markets, in the sites in classic northern Honduras, there is no evidence for mass consumption or centralized distribution. Instead, each village had its own production, and while the images produced by different molds were similar, there is no evidence of production of many duplicates from the same mold. So, she asked, why would these people be using molds to make their figurines, if they were not concerned to make many copies of each one?

Her alternative suggestion comes from thinking about the crafting of figurines as a social activity. Both animal and human subjects were made, and the human subjects include both males and females. Among the humans, the majority that she excavated were females, shown engaged in a small range of activities (see fig. 11). Many of the female figurines held pots, some with round balls as their contents. Others showed children being suckled or dandled on the knees of an adult woman. Males in figurines from her sites, and from collections at other neighboring villages, were often shown wearing animal heads as helmets or hats. One unique example of a figurine of this kind, excavated at the contemporary site of Cerro Palenque, south of the villages explored by Lopiparo, wore a feathered costume and held a musical instrument in his hand.[12]

Lopiparo suggested that the human subjects depicted in figurines were men and women shown as contributors to the reproduction of their social group. She demonstrated a close association between the rebuilding of houses, the burial of the dead in household settings, and the use of figurines. Shaping clay into human form, like reshaping the building where the family lived, was linked to reshaping the social group, as the dead became ancestors.

Molding served as a technology that allowed anyone, regardless of skill, to produce an image that was recognizable and that represented the contributions of different people to the social group. Lopiparo suggested that children would have been especially important participants in the crafting of figurines, learning how to be members of their society through their participation in the shaping of these conventionalized images. Exposed to imagery that celebrated women's contributions to child-rearing and food-serving, as much as or more than male participation in masked rituals, children in these villages, she suggests, learned without words that both men and women were important.

Feminist archaeology makes a difference

Lopiparo's analysis is explicitly grounded in feminist thought. She draws on analogies with the ethnographic observations of an Amazonian society in Ecuador by archaeologist Brenda Bowser. Bowser's work explores the way that women's actions, making pottery serving vessels, brewing alcoholic beverages, and serving them to visitors to their homes, are political.[13] In the village Bowser studied, alliances among different families were negotiated in conversations that took place on such visits, and cemented through the hospitality that visiting men accepted from the members of the host household.

If we viewed this Amazonian ethnographic situation without the insights gained from feminist anthropological work, we might make the mistake of seeing women as "restricted" to the home, and men as the only political actors, with politics defined as the speeches and alliances evident in public spaces outside the houses. Instead, Bowser showed ethnographically that the kinds of arguments advanced by archaeologists such as Julia Hendon are correct. Household activities have to be treated as political action; even if women were ever limited in action to households (a dubious generalization) they would still be affecting the course of their societies.[14]

Lopiparo provides all the pieces to imagine the scenes of daily life in farming villages of Classic northern Honduras. In houses throughout the village, men, women, and children could be found pursuing their own unique courses of action. Some of the activities underway might have been similar from one house to another: food might be cooking, craftwork might be underway, maintenance tasks might be in process around the house and yard. What any one person was doing would partly depend on the household in which they lived. Some households might include individual men or women recognized as especially talented in medical practice, in rituals of divination, or in specific craftwork. In others, all the time of the residents might have been taken up with tasks related to farming. In a very few households, visitors from more distant places might be found, or members of the household might themselves be away, traveling to other towns. Some of the people in any house might be practicing music, dances or games they would take part in at upcoming festivals.

Far from the impoverished stereotypes that archaeology provides when it does not actively consider the differences among people living in the past, even small villages provided ample opportunity for each person's life experience to be distinct from that of others of the same age, sex, or social status. More than this: it was through the materially mediated experience of difference and identification that any person developed a sense of who they were in their society, including how they experienced their biological sex.

The children in households producing figurines would have learned through their participation in this process of representation not just what men and women were like, but the value placed by their families and neighbors on certain ways of being male and female. Both the figurines, and the older people with whom they were working when making them, provided models for young people in their own performance of gender. In Judith Butler's terms, figurines were precedents cited when children conformed their own actions to these models, perhaps even more powerful because the messages they conveyed were absorbed visually and tactilely, not just through words.

The objects crafted in these households were more than art-works. Many were also musical instruments, whistles or rattles. Once successfully fired, these could be brought out to accompany performances. Some of these performances took place on the occasion of the burial of older members of households, and the renovation of houses that seems to have closely followed some burials. Other performances likely took place to mark different life events, such as the moments when the ears of children were pierced the first time, or when they began to wear adult ear ornaments, the kind of event that produced the trash collected at Puerto Escondido, not far from where Lopiparo worked, around AD 400. Painted figurines and figural instruments may also have been used when unanticipated events happened, such as illness requiring the efforts of curers. Every time they were used, these objects published to all present valued images of human experience that reinforced without words the way that adult women and men contributed to social life. Simultaneously, these images were objects of the admiration that desire fueled and so contributed to the formation of sexuality among the people whose embodied performances they depicted.

Nor was it only the visual culture of these villages that helped produce differential experiences of bodily life that we would recognize as gender. Through their everyday experience of the spatial relations that the design of the house allowed, and that the layout of villages fostered, children learned and adults had reinforced their senses of appropriate spheres of action. The maps that archaeologists produce today show all the spatial features as if these were equally available and equally known to everyone in the past. In fact, each person's geographic circulation would have been unique, and the degree to which people of one sex shared such experiences cannot be taken for granted. In villages where men were the main agricultural labor force, and women were occupied in tasks in the home, the fields may have been a communal space that produced a shared experience specific to adult men. Women left in the village might have had no such sense of what it was to be part of a common group. Alternatively, men and women could have cooperated in the fields, making them a space where gender complementarity was materially produced. Or women who stayed in the village might have taken their tasks into outside spaces and worked together, sharing labor and talk. In any of these (or other) scenarios, shared activity in space, or different actions in the same place, contributed to creating distinctions in lived experiences among people through which any categorical gender difference that might have been proposed was given a sense of reality.

The future of archaeologies of sex and gender

We cannot take for granted that differences in experience in the past always were divided on the basis of sex, let alone that sex differences were understood as a simple binary. But we can ask how people in the past might have experienced their differences, including sex, throughout their life, and through their engagement with the material worlds they shared with others. Those material worlds, including representations in text and images, remain as traces of past experiences that archaeologists have developed skills to interpret. If there is one thing that the decades of effort in archaeologies of gender have taught us, it is that no material trace lacks the potential to speak to gendered experience. It is through the juxtaposition of different traces that archaeologists have come to see how their own biases, overlaid on stereotyped perspectives of people in past societies, can make it hard for us to see the truly original contribution of past lives to our present understandings.

So, while we may expect that images of women and men will continue to dominate the way we think about gender and sex in the past, we need to approach these visual documents aware that our own history of a two-sex model may lead us to assign all human images to two categories and thus miss other ways of conceiving of human difference. Even when we are examining the remains of human bodies, we must acknowledge that a large proportion, including all the children and youths, cannot be divided into two categories, and that even if we could do so, differences we see may owe more to other factors than sex/gender. While exploration of the tools, residues, and products of labor will no doubt continue to be important sources for identifying times and places when different kinds of people habitually performed different tasks, we must avoid assuming that those divisions of labor conformed to our ideas of sex, and that women's and men's work were always ranked in importance.

The products of future archaeologies of gender and sex will not be quite the same as those that have gained favor in gender studies in the past. While the way that violence was structured by sex may continue to absorb our interests, simple identifications of Amazons and male warriors should be examined with suspicion, as reflections of modern gender ideologies. Finding how and where women held political power will continue to be of interest, but documenting the existence of queens will not substitute for understanding the intersections of power and difference throughout society. Figurines and other self-representations will serve us well as potential clues to concerns with shaping of the self and social relations, rather than as straightforward evidence of goddess worship or peaceful matriarchy.

Producing richer, more complicated views of pasts vastly different than today will need to draw on all the strengths of archaeology. By insisting that the specific spatial and historical context of the traces of past human lives matters, we will continue to avoid generalizing local lives as uniform human life. By pursuing all the kinds of evidence that can be developed from even the most unprepossessing sites we will build up a scrupulously detailed image of material constraints and possibilities experienced by people at different points in time.

But it is not in such methodological approaches that archaeologies of sex and gender distinguish themselves. Rather, it is in beginning philosophical commitments that we share with other students of sex and gender: to acknowledge that our own position in society and history influences how we understand the past; to respect human dignity, including the dignity of people unlike ourselves; and to combat attempts to maintain inequalities in the contemporary world in every way possible.

For the latter purpose, the past is a powerful resource. When it is offered as simply the precedent for the inevitable reproduction of sexual inequality, everyone committed to oppose inequality should question what is being said. In order to claim the right to combat such uses of the past, it is equally necessary for us to critique our own positions and to try, as far as possible, not to reproduce the same interpretive violence. Archaeological materialities resist reduction, break through overly simple models, and force us to confront our own least interrogated assumptions. Archaeology promises something that we think is a powerful tool for students of gender: a past in which inequality on the basis of sex was not inevitable, and thus is not a natural and unavoidable feature of contemporary life.

Notes

Bibliographical references given in
abbreviated form in the Notes are
given in full in the Bibliography.

Introduction

1   Barstow 1978; Gimbutas 1982, 1989, 1991; see
    also Conkey and Tringham 1995; Dobres
    1992; Meskell 1995, 1998b; Nelson 1990;
    Russell 1993; Tringham and Conkey 1998.
2   Trinkhaus and Svoboda 2006.
3   Kralik, Novotny, and Oliva 2002; Soffer,
    Vandiver, Klima, and Svoboda 1993;
    Vandiver, Soffer, Klima, and Svoboda
    1989, 1990.
4   Soffer 2004; Soffer, Adovasio, and Hyland
    2000.
5   Conkey 1997; Soffer 1997.
6   Soffer, Adovasio, and Hyland 2000.
7   Ibid.
8   Ibid.
9   Soffer and Conkey 1997.
10 Meade and Wiesner-Hanks (eds) 2004;
    Phillips and Reay (eds) 2002.
11 Isaac 1978; Potts 1984; Power and Watts 1996;
    Tanner and Zihlman 1976; Zihlman 1978,
    1981; see also Conkey and Williams 1991;
    Fedigan 1986; Hager 1997.
12 Foucault 1978; Gimbutas 1982, 1989, 1991;
    Laqueur 1990.
13 Exceptions include Conkey and Tringham
    1995; Conkey and Williams 1991; Dobres
    2004; Hays-Gilpin 2000; Joyce 2004b;
    Spector and Whalen 1989.
14 Trigger 2006.
15 Preucel and Hodder 1996; Meskell
    and Preucel 2004; Wylie 2002.
16 Brumfiel 1992; Wylie 1991, 2002.
17 Flannery and Winter 1976.
18 Spector 1983; Conkey and Spector 1984;
    Weedman 2004.
19 Hendon 1996, 2004, 2006a; MacEachern,
    Archer, and Garvin 1989; Wilk and Rathje
    1982; Wilk and Ashmore 1988.

20 Arnold, Gilchrist, Graves, and Taylor 1988;
    Bertelsen, Lillehammer, and Naess 1987;
    Claassen 1992; Conkey and Gero 1991;
    Conkey and Spector 1984; duCros and
    Smith 1993; Engelstad 1991; Gilchrist
    1991; Hodder 1984; Nelson 1993; Spector
    1983; Walde and Willows 1991; see also
    Conkey and Gero 1997; Gilchrist 1999;
    Hays-Gilpin 2000; Joyce 2004a; Wilkie
    and Hayes 2006.
21 See individual contributions in Nelson
    2006.
22 Contrast Sørensen 2000 with Brumfiel
    2006; Gilchrist 1991, 1999; Wylie 1992, 1996.
23 Joyce and Claassen 1997:1.

Chapter 1

1   Joyce and Henderson 2001; Joyce 2000a,
    2001c, 2003a, 2003b.
2   Black and Jolly 2003; Hodder 1999; Joyce
    2002c; Lucas 2001; Praetzellis 2000.
3   Henderson and Joyce 2004.
4   Schiffer 1987; Richards and Thomas 1984;
    Hoskins 2006.
5   Jones 2004.
6   Joyce, Shackley, McCandless, and
    Sheptak 2004.
7   Luke, Joyce, Henderson and Tykot 2003.
8   Lopiparo 2006; Lopiparo, Joyce, and
    Hendon 2005.
9   For example, Ambrose, Buikstra, and
    Krueger 2003; Cohen and Bennett 1993;
    Cox and Sealy 1997; Gerry and Chesson
    2000; White, Storey, Longstaffe, and
    Spence 2004.
10 Robin 2002.
11 Hastorf 1991.
12 Spector 1983; Conkey and Spector 1984;
    compare Dobres 1995; Wylie 1992.
13 Stahl 1993; Wylie 1985, 1988, 2002.
14 Moore 1988, 1994.
15 Hendon 1997, 1999a, 2002, 2006b;
    Robin 2006.

16 See Pyburn 2004 for a critique of these assumptions.

17 Weston 1993.

18 Fausto-Sterling 2000; Roughgarden 2004.

19 For general critiques, see Butler 1990, 1993, 2004; Grosz 1995; for anthropology, see Moore 1988, 1994; for archaeology, Joyce 2004a; Meskell 2005.

Chapter 2

1 Covarrubias 1950, 1957; Porter 1953.

2 Griffin 1972:307–309; Roosevelt 1987; contrast Lesure 2002.

3 Garcia Moll *et al.* 1991; Piña Chan 1958.

4 Tolstoy 1989.

5 Serra and Sugiura 1987; Tolstoy 1989.

6 Garcia Moll *et al.* 1991; Joyce 1999, 2001a, 2002a, 2002c.

7 Arnold 2006:143; compare Fausto-Sterling 2000; Geller 2005; Hollimon 2006:441–43.

8 Joyce 1999, 2001a, 2002a.

9 Bruhns 1988; Freidel and Schele 2001; Hendon 1997, 1999a, 1999b, 2002; Joyce 1992, 1993, 1996, 2001c; McAnany and Plank 2001; Marcus 1992, 2001; Stone 1988; Sweely 1998, 1999.

10 Dobres 1992; Russell 1993.

11 McCoid and McDermott 1996; McDermott 1996; Rice 1987.

12 Barstow 1978; Gimbutas 1982, 1989, 1991.

13 Cited in Roscoe 1991:50.

14 Blackwood 1984; Callender and Kochems 2000; Jacobs, Thomas, and Lang 1996; Roscoe 1998.

15 For example, Whitehead 1981.

16 Hollimon 2006; Perry and Joyce 2001; Voss 2006:375–77.

17 Hollimon 1991, 1997, 2000a.

18 Hollimon 1997; see also Hollimon 2000a:189; Schmidt 2000.

19 Hollimon 1997:186.

20 Hollimon 2000a.

21 Hollimon 2000b, 2001.

22 Lang 1998: 303–308; Medicine 1983; Midnight Sun 1988:41–45.

23 Lang 1998: 276–79; Medicine 1983.

24 Prine 2000.

25 Conkey 1991.

26 Conkey 1997; Conkey and Tringham 1995; Soffer and Conkey 1997; Tringham and Conkey 1998.

Chapter 3

1 Freidel and Schele 2001; see also Martin and Grube 2000.

2 Taylor 1948.

3 For an overview of Maya archaeology, see Henderson 1997.

4 Compare Tozzer 1941 with Seler 1923.

5 Proskouriakoff 1960, 1963, 1964.

6 Proskouriakoff 1961.

7 Martin and Grube 2000.

8 Marcus 1976.

9 Coggins 1975.

10 Fox and Justeson 1986; Haviland 1977; Hopkins 1988; Joyce 1981; Thompson 1982; see also Gillespie 2000; Robin 2001.

11 MacCormack and Strathern 1980; Ortner and Whitehead 1981; Rosaldo and Lamphere (eds) 1974; Yanagisako and Collier (eds) 1987.

12 Davis-Kimball 1997a, 1997b, 1997c; 2002.

13 Arnold 1991; Arnold 2002:252–54; Arnold 2006:152–55.

14 Ardren 2002; Freidel and Schele 2001; Martin and Grube 2000; McAnany and Plank 2001.

15 Exceptions include Freter 2004; Pyburn 1998; Robin 2002; Sweely 1998, 1999; Webster and Gonlin 1988.

16 For example, at Copán: Hendon 1997, 1999a, 2002; Storey 1998.

17 Robin 2003; see also Fung 1995; Hendon 1997, 2002; Lopiparo 2006; Pyburn 1998; Robin 2002, 2006; Sweely 1998, 1999.

18 Ruscheinsky 1995.

19 Krochock 1991, 2002.

20 Inomata 2001.

21 Robin 2006.

22 Goldberg 1999; Nevett 1994; Spencer-Wood 2006.

23 Laqueur 1990.
24 Goldberg 1999; Nevett 1994; Ridgway 1987; Walker 1983.

Chapter 4

1 Yates 1993.
2 Joyce 2000a, 2001b, 2002a; Sigal 2005, 2007.
3 Weston 1993.
4 Meskell 2005.
5 Joyce 2000a, 2001b; McCafferty and McCafferty 1999; Sigal 2005, 2007.
6 Treherne 1995.
7 Hendon 1997, 1999a, 1999b, 2002, 2006b; McAnany and Plank 2001; McCafferty and McCafferty 1991.
8 Joyce 2000a; McCafferty and McCafferty 1991.
9 Brumbach and Jarvenpa 2006:520–22; Cohen and Bennett 1993; Hollimon 2000b, 2001; Perry 2004.
10 Cohen and Bennett 1993.
11 Brumbach and Jarvenpa 2006:520–22; Hollimon 1991.
12 Hollimon 1997.
13 McAnany and Plank 2001; Reents-Budet 1994.
14 McNeill 2007; Reents-Budet 1994.
15 Bachand, Joyce and Hendon 2003; Butler 1990, 1993, 2004; Perry and Joyce 2001; Joyce 2004a, 2005.
16 Joyce 1992, 1993, 1996, 2000b, 2001b, 2001c, 2002b.
17 Klein 2001.
18 Proskouriakoff 1960, 1961.
19 Marcus 1976, 1992, 2001.
20 Bruhns 1988.
21 Bassie-Sweet 2002; Joyce 1996; Looper 2002; Reilly 2002; Stone 1991; Taube 1985.
22 Joyce 2000b, 2002b.
23 Meskell 1999; 2000b.
24 Voss 2000.
25 Joyce 2000b.
26 Stone 1988, 1995.
27 Pillsbury 2001.
28 Bergh 1993; Gero 2004.

29 Weismantel 2004.
30 Brumfiel 1991, 1996, 2001; Evans 1998, 2001; Overholtzer 2005; Joyce 2000a, 2001b.
31 Joyce 2000a, 2001b.
32 Burkhart 1997.
33 McCafferty and McCafferty 1988.
34 Gilchrist 1994, 2000.
35 Costello 2000; Crist 2005; Gilfoyle 2005; Ketz, Abel, and Schmidt 2005; Meyer, Gibson, and Costello 2005; O'Brien 2005; Seifert 1991; Seifert, O'Brien, and Balicki 2000; Seifert and Balicki 2005; Spude 2005; Yamin 2005.
36 O'Brien 2005; Seifert 1991; Seifert, O'Brien, and Balicki 2000; Seifert and Balicki 2005.
37 Costello 2000; Meyer, Gibson, and Costello 2005.
38 Costello 2000; Crist 2005; Ketz, Abel, and Schmidt 2005; Meyer, Gibson, and Costello 2005; Yamin 2005.
39 Gilchrist 2000; Grosz 1995.

Chapter 5

1 Wilkie 2003; Wilkie and Shorter 2001.
2 Wilkie 2003:105; see also 103–109.
3 Hastorf 1991.
4 Geller 2005.
5 White 2005.
6 Cohen and Bennett 1993.
7 Hollimon 2001.
8 Agarwal 2001; Agarwal, Dumitriu, Tomlinson, and Grynpas 2004.
9 Meskell 1998a, 1999, 2000a, 2000b.
10 Fung 1995.
11 Lopiparo 2006.
12 Joyce 1993.
13 Bowser 2000, 2004.
14 Hendon 1996, 2004, 2006a.

Bibliography

Agarwal, Sabrina C. 2001. "The Influence of Age and Sex on Trabecular Architecture and Bone Mineral Density in Three British Historical Populations," Ph.D. dissertation, University of Toronto.

Agarwal, Sabrina C., Mircea Dumitriu, George A. Tomlinson, and Marc D. Grynpas 2004. "Medieval trabecular bone architecture: The influence of age, sex, and lifestyle," *American Journal of Physical Anthropology* 124:33–44.

Ambrose, Stanley H., Jane Buikstra, and Harold W. Krueger 2003. "Status and gender differences in diet at Mound 72, Cahokia, revealed by isotopic analysis of bone," *Journal of Anthropological Archaeology* 22:217–26.

Ardren, Traci (ed.) 2002. *Ancient Maya Women*, Walnut Creek, CA: AltaMira Press.

Arnold, Bettina 1991. "The deposed Princess of Vix: The need for an engendered European prehistory," in *The Archaeology of Gender: Proceedings of the 22nd Annual Chacmool Conference*, Dale Walde and Noreen Willows (eds), pp. 366–74, Calgary: Department of Archaeology, University of Calgary.

— 2002. "'Sein und werden': Gender as process in mortuary ritual," in *In Pursuit of Gender*, Sarah Nelson and Myriam Rosen-Ayalon (eds), pp. 239–56, Walnut Creek, CA: AltaMira Press.

— 2006. "Gender and archaeological mortuary analysis," in *Handbook of Gender in Archaeology*, Sarah Nelson (ed.), pp. 137–70, Lanham, MD: AltaMira Press.

Arnold, Karen, Roberta Gilchrist, Pam Graves, and Sarah Taylor (eds) 1988. *Women in Archaeology*, theme issue of *Archaeological Reviews from Cambridge* 7 (1).

Bachand, Holly, Rosemary A. Joyce, and Julia A. Hendon 2003. "Bodies moving in space: Ancient Mesoamerican human sculpture and embodiment," *Cambridge Archaeological Journal* 13 (2):238–47.

Barstow, Ann 1978. "The uses of archaeology for women's history: James Mellaart's work on the Neolithic Goddess at Çatal Hüyük," *Feminist Studies* 4:7–17.

Bassie-Sweet, Karen 2002. "Corn Deities and the Male/Female Principle," in *Ancient Maya Gender Identity and Relations*, Lowell Gustafson and Amy Trevelyan (eds), pp. 169–90, Westport, CT: Greenwood Press.

Bergh, Susan E. 1993. "Death and renewal in Moche phallic-spouted vessels," *Res* 24:78–94.

Bertelsen, Reidar, Arvid Lillehammer, and Jenny-Rita Naess (eds) 1987. *Were They All Men? An Examination of Sex Roles in Prehistoric Society*, Stavanger, Norway: Arkeologist Museum i Stavanger.

Black, Stephen L., and Kevin Jolly 2003. *Archaeology by Design*, Walnut Creek, CA: AltaMira Press.

Blackwood, Evelyn 1984. "Sexuality and gender in certain Native American tribes: The case of cross-gender females," *Signs* 10:27–42.

Bowser, Brenda J. 2000. "From pottery to politics: An ethnoarchaeological study of political factionalism, ethnicity, and domestic pottery style in the Ecuadorian Amazon," *Journal of Archaeological Method and Theory* 7(3):219–48.

— 2004. "Domestic spaces as public places: An ethnoarchaeological case study of houses, gender, and politics in the Ecuadorian Amazon," *Journal of Archaeological Method and Theory* 11(2):157–81.

Bruhns, Karen Olsen 1988. "Yesterday the Queen Wore...An Analysis of Women and Costume in Public Art of the Late Classic Maya," in *The Role of Gender in Precolumbian Art and Architecture*, Virginia Miller (ed.), pp. 105–34, Lanham, MD: University Press of America.

Brumbach, Hetty Jo, and Robert Jarvenpa 2006. "Gender dynamics in hunter-gatherer society: Archaeological methods and perspectives," in *Handbook of Gender in Archaeology*, Sarah Nelson (ed.), pp. 503–35, Lanham, MD: AltaMira Press.

Brumfiel, Elizabeth 1991. "Weaving and cooking: Women's production in Aztec Mexico," in *Engendering Archaeology*, Margaret Conkey and Joan Gero (eds), pp. 224–51, Oxford: Blackwell.

— 1992. "Distinguished lecture in archaeology: Breaking and entering the ecosystem: gender, class, and faction steal the show," *American Anthropologist* 94:551–67.

— 1996. "Figurines and the Aztec state: Testing the effectiveness of ideological domination," in *Gender and Archaeology*, Rita Wright (ed.), pp. 143–66, Philadelphia: University of Pennsylvania Press.

— 2001. "Asking about Aztec gender: The historical and archaeological evidence," in *Gender in Pre-Hispanic America*, Cecelia Klein (ed.), pp. 57–85, Washington, DC: Dumbarton Oaks.

— 2006. "Methods in feminist and gender archaeology: A feeling for difference – and likeness," in *Handbook of Gender in Archaeology*, Sarah Nelson (ed.), pp. 31–58, Lanham, MD: AltaMira Press.

Burkhart, Louise M. 1997. "Mexica women on the 'home front': Housework and religion in Aztec Mexico," in *Indian Women of Early Mexico*, Susan Schroeder, Stephanie Wood, and Robert Haskett (eds), pp. 25–54, Norman: University of Oklahoma Press.

Butler, Judith 1990. *Gender Trouble: Feminism and the Subversion of Identity*, New York: Routledge.

— 1993. *Bodies that Matter: On the Discursive Limits of 'Sex'*, New York: Routledge.

— 2004. *Undoing Gender*, New York: Routledge.

Callender, Charles, and Lee M. Kochems 2000. "The North American berdache," *Current Anthropology* 24:443–70.

Claassen, Cheryl (ed.) 1992. *Exploring Gender through Archaeology*, Madison, WI: Prehistory Press.

Coggins, Clemency C. 1975. "Painting and Drawing Styles at Tikal: An Historical and Iconographic Reconstruction," Ph.D. dissertation, Department of Art History, Harvard University. Ann Arbor: University Microfilms.

Cohen, Mark, and Sharon Bennett 1993. "Skeletal evidence for sex roles and gender hierarchies in prehistory," in *Sex and Gender Hierarchies*, Barbara Miller (ed.), pp. 273–96, Cambridge: Cambridge University Press.

Conkey, Margaret W. 1991. "Contexts of action, contexts for power: Material culture and gender in the Magdalenian," in *Engendering Archaeology*, Margaret W. Conkey and Joan Gero (eds), pp. 57–92, Oxford: Blackwell.

— 1997. "Beyond art and between the caves: Thinking about context in the interpretive process," in *Beyond Art: Pleistocene Image and Symbol*, Margaret Conkey, Olga Soffer, Deborah Statmann, and Nina Jablonksi (eds), pp. 343–67, San Francisco: California Academy of Sciences and University of California Press.

Conkey, Margaret W., and Joan Gero (eds) 1991. *Engendering Archaeology: Women and Prehistory*, Oxford: Blackwell.

Conkey, Margaret W., and Joan Gero 1997. "Programme to practice: gender and feminism in archaeology," *Annual Review of Anthropology* 26:411–37.

Conkey, Margaret W., and Janet Spector 1984. "Archaeology and the study of gender," *Advances in Archaeological Method and Theory* 7:1–38.

Conkey, Margaret W., and Ruth E. Tringham 1995. "Archaeology and the goddess: Exploring the contours of feminist archaeology," in *Feminism in the Academy*, Domna C. Stanton and Abigail J. Stewart (eds), pp. 199–247, Ann Arbor: University of Michigan Press.

Haviland, William A. 1977. "Dynastic genealogies from Tikal, Guatemala: Implications for descent and political organization," *American Antiquity* 42:61–67.

Hays-Gilpin, Kelley 2000. "Feminist scholarship in archaeology," *Annals of the American Academy of Political and Social Sciences* 571:89–106.

Henderson, John S. 1997. *The World of the Ancient Maya*, second edition, Ithaca: Cornell University Press.

Henderson, John S., and Rosemary A. Joyce 2004. "Human use of animals in prehispanic Honduras: A preliminary report from the lower Ulúa Valley, Honduras," in *Maya Zooarchaeology: New Directions in Theory and Method*, Kitty F. Emery (ed.), pp. 223–36, Monograph 51, Los Angeles: UCLA Institute of Archaeology.

Hendon, Julia A. 1996. "Archaeological approaches to the organization of domestic labor: Household practice and domestic relations," *Annual Review of Anthropology* 25:45–61.

— 1997. "Women's work, women's space, and women's status among the Classic-Period Maya elite of the Copán Valley, Honduras," in *Women in Prehistory: North America and Mesoamerica*, Cheryl Claassen and Rosemary A. Joyce (eds), pp. 33–46, Philadelphia: University of Pennsylvania Press.

— 1999a. "Multiple Sources of Prestige and the Social Evaluation of Women in Prehispanic Mesoamerica," in *Material Symbols: Culture and Economy in Prehistory*, John Robb (ed.), pp. 257–76, Occasional Paper 26, Carbondale: Center for Archaeological Investigations, Southern Illinois University.

— 1999b. "Spinning and weaving in Pre-Hispanic Mesoamerica: The technology and social relations of textile production." in *Mayan Clothing and Weaving through the Ages*, Barbara Knoke de Arathoon, Nancie L. Gonzalez, and John M. Willemsen Devlin (eds), pp. 7–16, Guatemala City: Museo Ixchel del Traje Indígena.

— 2002. "Household and state in Pre-Hispanic Maya society: Gender, identity, and practice," in *Ancient Maya Gender Identity and Relations*, Lowell Gustafson and Amy Trevelyan (eds), pp. 75–92, Westport, CT: Greenwood Press.

— 2004. "Living and working at home: The social archaeology of household production and social relations," in *A Companion to Social Archaeology*, Lynn M. Meskell and Robert W. Preucel (eds), pp. 272–86, Malden, MA: Blackwell.

— 2006a. "The engendered household," in *Handbook of Gender in Archaeology*, Sarah Nelson (ed.), pp. 171–98, Lanham, MD: AltaMira Press.

— 2006b. "Textile production as craft in Mesoamerica: Time, labor and knowledge," *Journal of Social Archaeology* 6:354–78.

Hodder, Ian 1984. "Burials, houses, women and men in the European Neolithic," in *Ideology, Power, and Prehistory*, Daniel Miller and Christopher Tilley (eds), pp. 51–68, Cambridge: Cambridge University Press.

— 1999. *The Archaeological Process*, Oxford: Blackwell.

Hollimon, Sandra E. 1991. "Health consequences of the division of labor among the Chumash Indians of Southern California," in *The Archaeology of Gender: Proceedings of the 22nd Annual Chacmool Conference*, Dale Walde and Noreen D. Willows (eds), pp. 462–69, Calgary: Department of Archaeology, Calgary University.

— 1997. "The third gender in native California: Two-spirit undertakers among the Chumash and their neighbors," in *Women in Prehistory: North America and Mesoamerica*, Cheryl Claassen and Rosemary A. Joyce (eds), pp. 173–88, Philadelphia: University of Pennsylvania Press.

— 2000a. "Archaeology of the 'aqi: gender and sexuality in prehistoric Chumash society," in *Archaeologies of Sexuality*, Robert A.

Schmidt and Barbara L. Voss (eds), pp. 179–96, London: Routledge.

— 2000b. "Sex, health and gender roles among the Arikara of the Northern Plains," in *Reading the Body: Representations and Remains in the Archaeological Record*, Alison Rautman (ed.), pp. 25–37, Philadelphia: University of Pennsylvania Press.

— 2001. "Warfare and gender in the northern Plains: Osteological evidence of trauma reconsidered," in *Gender and the Archaeology of Death*, Bettina Arnold and Nancy Wicker (eds), pp. 179–93, Walnut Creek, CA: AltaMira Press.

— 2006. "The archaeology of nonbinary genders in Native North America," in *Handbook of Gender in Archaeology*, Sarah Nelson (ed.), pp. 435–50, Lanham, MD: AltaMira Press.

Hopkins, Nicholas A. 1988. "Classic Maya kinship systems: Epigraphic and ethnographic evidence for patrilineality," *Estudios de Cultura Maya* 17:87–121.

Hoskins, Janet 2006. "Agency, Biography and Objects," in *Handbook of Material Culture*, Christopher Tilley, Webb Keane, Susanne Kuechler-Fogden, Mike Rowlands, and Patricia Spyer (eds), pp. 74–84, Thousand Oaks, CA: SAGE Publications.

Inomata, Takeshi 2001. "Power and ideology of artistic creation: Elite craft specialists in Classic Maya society," *Current Anthropology* 42 (3):321–49.

Isaac, Glynn L. 1978. "Foodsharing and human evolution: Archaeological evidence from the Plio-Pleistocene of South Africa," *Journal of Archaeological Research* 34:311–25.

Jacobs, Sue-Ellen, Wesley Thomas, and Sabine Lang (eds) 1996. *Two-Spirit People: Native American Gender Identity, Sexuality, and Spirituality*, Urbana: University of Illinois Press.

Jones, Andrew 2004. "Archaeometry and materiality: Materials-based analysis in theory and practice," *Archaeometry* 46:327–38.

Joyce, Rosemary A. 1981. "Classic Maya kinship and descent: An alternative suggestion," *Journal of the Steward Anthropological Society* 13:45–57.

— 1992. "Dimensiones simbolicas del traje en monumentos clasicos Mayas: La construccion del genero a traves del vestido," in *La Indumentaria y el Tejido Mayas a Traves del Tiempo*, Linda Asturias and Dina Fernandez (eds), pp. 29–38, Guatemala: Museo Ixchel del Traje Indígena.

— 1993. "Women's work: Images of production and reproduction in Prehispanic Southern Central America," *Current Anthropology* 34 (3):255–74.

— 1996. "The construction of gender in Classic Maya monuments," in *Gender in Archaeology*, Rita Wright (ed.), pp. 167–95, Philadelphia: University of Pennsylvania Press.

— 1999. "Social dimensions of Pre-Classic burials," in *Social Patterns in Pre-Classic Mesoamerica*, David C. Grove and Rosemary A. Joyce (eds), pp. 15–47, Washington, DC: Dumbarton Oaks.

— 2000a. "Girling the girl and boying the boy: The production of adulthood in ancient Mesoamerica, *World Archaeology* 31:473–83.

— 2000b. "A Precolumbian gaze: Male sexuality among the Ancient Maya," in *Archaeologies of Sexuality*, Robert A. Schmidt and Barbara L. Voss (eds), pp. 263–83, London: Routledge.

— 2001a. "Burying the dead at Tlatilco: Social memory and social identities," in *New Perspectives on Mortuary Analysis*, Meredith Chesson (ed.), pp. 12–26, Archaeology Division of the American Anthropological Association, Monograph 10, Alexandria, VA: American Anthropological Association.

— 2001b. *Gender and Power in Prehispanic Mesoamerica*, Austin: University of Texas Press.

— 2001c. "Negotiating sex and gender in Classic Maya society," in *Gender in Pre-Hispanic America*, Cecelia Klein (ed.), pp. 109–41, Washington, DC: Dumbarton Oaks.

— 2002a. "Beauty, sexuality, body ornamentation and gender in Ancient Mesoamerica," in *In Pursuit of Gender*, Sarah Nelson and Myriam Rosen-Ayalon (eds), pp. 81–92, Walnut Creek, CA: AltaMira Press.

— 2002b. "Desiring women: Classic Maya sexualities," in *Ancient Maya Gender Identity and Relations*, Lowell Gustafson and Amelia Trevelyan (eds), pp. 329–44, Westport, CT: Greenwood Publishing.

— 2002c. *The Languages of Archaeology*, Oxford: Blackwell.

— 2003a. "Concrete memories: Fragments of the past in the Classic Maya present (500–1000 AD)," in *Archaeologies of Memory*, Ruth Van Dyke and Susan Alcock (eds), pp. 104–25, Malden, MA: Blackwell.

— 2003b. "Making something of herself: Embodiment in life and death at Playa de los Muertos, Honduras," *Cambridge Archaeological Journal* 13:248–61.

— 2004a. "Embodied subjectivity: Gender, femininity, masculinity, sexuality," in *A Companion to Social Archaeology*, Lynn M. Meskell and Robert W. Preucel (eds), pp. 82–95, Oxford: Blackwell.

— 2004b. "Gender in the Ancient Americas: From earliest villages to European colonization," in *A Companion to Gender History*, Teresa A. Meade and Merry E. Wiesner-Hanks (eds), pp. 305–20, Malden, MA: Blackwell.

— 2005. "Archaeology of the body," *Annual Reviews in Anthropology* 34:139–58.

Joyce, Rosemary A., and Cheryl Claassen 1997. "Women in the ancient Americas: Archaeologists, gender, and the making of prehistory," in *Women in Prehistory: North America and Mesoamerica*, Cheryl Claassen and Rosemary A. Joyce (eds), pp. 1–14, Philadelphia: University of Pennsylvania Press.

Joyce, Rosemary A., and John S. Henderson 2001. "Beginnings of village life in eastern Mesoamerica," *Latin American Antiquity* 12:5–23.

Joyce, Rosemary A., M. Steven Shackley, Kenneth McCandless, and Russell N. Sheptak 2004. "Resultados preliminares de una investigación con EDXRF de obsidiana de Puerto Escondido," in *Memoria del VII Seminario de Antropología de Honduras "Dr. George Hasemann,"* Kevin Avalos (ed.), pp. 115–29, Tegucigalpa: Instituto Hondureño de Antropología e Historia.

Ketz, K. Anne, Elizabeth J. Abel, and Andrew J. Schmidt 2005. "Public images and private reality: An analysis of differentiation in a 19th century St. Paul bordello," *Historical Archaeology* 39 (1):74–88.

Klein, Cecelia 2001. "None of the above: Gender ambiguity in Nahua ideology," in *Gender in Pre-Hispanic America*, Cecelia Klein (ed.), pp. 183–253, Washington, DC: Dumbarton Oaks.

Kralik, Miroslav, Vladimir Novotny, and Martin Oliva 2002. "Fingerprint on the venus of Dolní Vèstonice I," *Anthropologie* 40:107–13.

Krochock, Ruth 1991. "Dedication ceremonies at Chichén Itzá: The glyphic evidence," in *Sixth Palenque Round Table, 1986*, Merle Green Robertson and Virginia M. Fields (eds), pp. 43–50, Norman: University of Oklahoma Press.

— 2002. "Women in the Hieroglyphic Inscriptions of Chichén Itzá," in *Ancient Maya Women*, Traci Ardren (ed.), pp. 152–70, Walnut Creek, CA: AltaMira Press.

Lang, Sabine 1998. *Men as Women, Women as Men: Changing Gender in Native American Cultures*, John L. Vantine (trans.), Austin: University of Texas Press.

Laqueur, Thomas W. 1990. *Making Sex: Body and Gender from the Greeks to Freud*, Cambridge, MA: Harvard University Press.

Lesure, Richard G. 2002. "The goddess diffracted," *Current Anthropology* 43:587–610.

Looper, Matthew G. 2002. "Women-Men (and Men-Women): Classic Maya rulers and the third gender," in *Ancient Maya Women*, Traci Ardren (ed.), pp. 171–202, Walnut Creek, CA: AltaMira Press.

Lopiparo, Jeanne 2006. "Crafting children: Materiality, social memory, and the reproduction of Terminal Classic house societies in the Ulúa Valley, Honduras," in *The Social Experience of Childhood in Ancient Mesoamerica*, Traci Ardren and Scott Hutson (eds), pp. 133–68, Boulder: University Press of Colorado.

Lopiparo, Jeanne, Rosemary A. Joyce, and Julia Hendon 2005. "Pottery production in the Terminal Classic Ulúa Valley," in *Terminal Classic Socioeconomic Processes in the Maya Lowlands through a Ceramic Lens*, Sandra L. López Varela and Antonia Foias (eds), pp. 107–19, BAR International Series 1447, Oxford: British Archaeological Reports.

Lucas, Gavin 2001. *Critical Approaches to Fieldwork: Contemporary and Historical Archaeological Practice*, London: Routledge.

Luke, Christina, Rosemary A. Joyce, John S. Henderson, and Robert H. Tykot 2003. "Marble carving traditions in Honduras: Formative through Terminal Classic," in *ASMOSIA 6, Interdisciplinary Studies on Ancient Stone – Proceedings of the Sixth International Conference of the Association for the Study of Marble and Other Stones in Antiquity, Venice, June 15–18, 2000*, Lorenzo Lazzarini (ed.), pp. 485–96, Padova: Bottega d'Erasmo.

MacCormack, Carol, and Marilyn Strathern (eds) 1980. *Nature, Culture and Gender*, Cambridge: Cambridge University Press.

MacEachern, Scott, David Archer, and Richard D. Garvin (eds) 1989. *Households and Communities*, Proceedings of the 21st Annual Chacmool Conference, Calgary: Department of Archaeology, Calgary University.

McAnany, Patricia A., and Shannon Plank 2001. "Perspectives on actors, gender roles, and architecture at Classic Maya courts and households," in *Royal Courts of the Ancient Maya. Vol. 1: Theory, Comparison, and Synthesis*, Takeshi Inomata and Stephen D. Houston (eds), pp. 84–129, Boulder, CO: Westview.

McCafferty, Geoffrey, and Sharisse McCafferty 1999. "The metamorphosis of Xochiquetzal: A window on womanhood in Pre- and Post-Conquest Mexico," in *Manifesting Power: Gender and the Interpretation of Power in Archaeology*, Tracy Sweeley (ed.), pp. 103–25, London: Routledge.

McCafferty, Sharisse D., and Geoffrey G. McCafferty 1988. "Powerful Women and the Myth of Male Dominance in Aztec Society," *Archaeological Review from Cambridge* 7:45–59.

— 1991. "Spinning and weaving as female gender identity in Post-Classic Mexico," in *Textile Traditions of Mesoamerica and the Andes: An Anthology*, Janet C. Berlo, Margot Schevill, and Edward B. Dwyer (eds), pp. 19–44, New York: Garland.

McCoid, Catherine H., and LeRoy D. McDermott 1996. "Toward decolonizing gender: Female vision in the upper palaeolithic," *American Anthropologist* 98:319–26.

McNeill, Cameron (ed.) 2006. *Chocolate in Mesoamerica: A Cultural History of Cacao*, Gainsville: University of Florida Press.

McDermott, LeRoy 1996. "Self-representation in Upper Paleolithic female figurines," *Current Anthropology* 37:227–75.

Martin, Simon, and Nikolai Grube 2000. *Chronicle of the Maya Kings and Queens: Deciphering the Dynasties of the Ancient Maya*, London: Thames & Hudson.

Marcus, Joyce 1976. *Emblem and State in the Classic Maya Lowlands*, Washington, DC: Dumbarton Oaks.

— 1992. "Royal families, royal texts: Examples from the Zapotec and Maya," in *Mesoamerican Elites: An Archaeological Assessment*, Diane Z. Chase and Arlen F. Chase (eds), pp. 221–41, Norman: University of Oklahoma Press.

— 2001. "Breaking the glass ceiling: The strategies of royal women in ancient states," in *Gender in Pre-Hispanic America*, Cecelia

Klein (ed.), pp. 305–40, Washington, DC: Dumbarton Oaks.

Meade, Teresa A., and Merry E. Wiesner-Hanks (eds) 2004. *A Companion to Gender History*, Malden, MA: Blackwell.

Medicine, Beatrice 1983. "'Warrior Women' – Sex role alternatives for Plains Indian women," in *The Hidden Half: Studies of Plains Indian Women*, Patricia Albers and Beatrice Medicine (eds), pp. 267–80, Washington, DC: University Press of America.

Meskell, Lynn M. 1995. "Goddesses, gimbutas, and 'New Age' archaeology," *Antiquity* 69:74–86.

— 1998a. "Intimate archaeologies: The case of Kha and Merit," *World Archaeology* 29 (3):363–79.

— 1998b. "Running the gamut: Gender, girls, and goddesses," *American Journal of Archaeology* 102:181–85.

— 1999. "Archaeologies of life and death," *American Journal of Archaeology* 103 (2):181–99.

— 2000a. "Cycles of life and death: Narrative homology and archaeological realities," *World Archaeology* 31 (3):423–41.

— 2000b. "Re-em(bed)ding sex: Domesticity, sexuality, and ritual in New Kingdom Egypt," in *Archaeologies of Sexuality*, Robert A. Schmidt and Barbara L. Voss (eds), pp. 235–62, London: Routledge.

— 2005. "De/naturalizing gender in prehistory," in *Complexities: Beyond Nature and Nurture*, Susan McKinnon and Sydel Silverman (eds), pp. 157–75, Chicago: University of Chicago Press.

Meskell, Lynn M., and Robert W. Preucel (eds) 2004. *A Companion to Social Archaeology*, Malden, MA: Blackwell.

Meyer, Michael D., Erica S. Gibson, and Julia G. Costello 2005. "City of angels, city of sin: Archaeology in the Los Angeles red-light district, ca. 1900," *Historical Archaeology* 39 (1):107–25.

Midnight Sun 1988. "Sex/gender systems in Native North America," in *Living the Spirit*, Will Roscoe (ed.), pp. 32–47, New York: St. Martin's Press.

Moore, Henrietta L. 1988. *Feminism and Anthropology*, Cambridge: Polity Press.

— 1994. *A Passion for Difference: Essays in Anthropology and Gender*, Bloomington: Indiana University Press.

Nelson, Sarah M. 1990. "Diversity of the Upper Palaeolithic 'Venus' figurines and archeological mythology," in *Powers of Observation*, Sarah M. Nelson and Alice B. Kehoe (eds), pp. 11–22, Archaeological Papers of the American Anthropological Association, No. 2, Washington, DC: American Anthropological Association.

— 1993. "Gender hierarchy and the Queens of Silla," in *Sex and Gender Hierarchies*, Barbara Miller (ed.), pp. 297–315, Cambridge: Cambridge University Press.

Nelson, Sarah M. (ed.) 2006. *Handbook of Gender in Archaeology*, Lanham, MD: AltaMira Press.

Nevett, Lisa 1994. "Separation or seclusion? Towards an archaeological approach to investigating women in the Greek household in the fifth to third centuries BC," *Architecture and Order: Approaches to Social Space*, Michael Parker Pearson and Colin Richards (eds), pp. 98–112, London: Routledge.

O'Brien, Elizabeth B. 2005. "Illicit congress in the nation's capital: The history of Mary Ann Hall's brothel," *Historical Archaeology* 39 (1):47–58.

Ortner, Sherry, and Harriet Whitehead (eds) 1981. *Sexual Meanings: The Cultural Construction of Gender and Sexuality*, Cambridge: Cambridge University Press.

Overholtzer, Lisa Marie 2005. "The Kneeling Mexica Woman: Evidence for male domination or gender complementarity?" Senior honors thesis, Department of Anthropology, University of California, Berkeley.

Perry, Elizabeth M. 2004. "Bioarchaeology of gender and labor in the prehispanic

American Southwest," Ph.D. dissertation, University of Arizona.

Perry, Elizabeth M., and Rosemary A. Joyce 2001. "Providing a past for *Bodies that Matter*: Judith Butler's impact on the archaeology of gender," *International Journal of Sexuality and Gender Studies* 6 (1 and 2):63–76.

Phillips, Kim M., and Barry Reay (eds) 2002. *Sexualities in History: A Reader*, New York: Routledge.

Pillsbury, Joanne (ed.) 2001. *Moche Art and Archaeology in Ancient Peru*, Washington, DC: National Gallery of Art.

Piña Chan, Román 1958. *Tlatilco*, 2 vols, Serie Investigaciones, No. 1–2, Mexico, DF: Instituto Nacional de Antropología e Historia.

Porter, Muriel 1953. *Tlatilco and the pre-classic cultures of the New World*, Viking Fund Publications in Anthropology, No. 19, New York: Wenner-Gren Foundation for Anthropological Research.

Potts, Richard B. 1984. "Home bases and early hominids," *American Scientist* 72:338–47.

Power, Camilla, and Ian Watts 1996. "Female strategies and collective behaviour: The archaeology of earliest *Homo sapiens sapiens*," in *The Archaeology of Human Ancestry: Power, Sex and Tradition*, James Steele and Stephen Shennan (eds), pp. 306–30, London: Routledge.

Praetzellis, Adrian 2000. *Death by Theory*, Walnut Creek, CA: AltaMira Press.

Preucel, Robert W., and Ian Hodder (eds) 1996. *Contemporary Archaeology in Theory*, Oxford: Blackwell.

Prine, Elizabeth 2000. "Searching for third genders: Towards a prehistory of domestic space in Middle Missouri villages," in *Archaeologies of Sexuality*, Robert A. Schmidt and Barbara L. Voss (eds), pp. 197–219, London: Routledge.

Proskouriakoff, Tatiana 1960. "Historical implications of a pattern of dates at Piedras Negras, Guatemala," *American Antiquity* 25:454–75.

— 1961. "Portraits of women in Maya art," in *Essays in Pre-Columbian Art and Archaeology*, Samuel K. Lothrop (ed.), pp. 81–99, Cambridge, MA: Harvard University Press.

— 1963. "Historical data in the inscriptions of Yaxchilan, Part I," *Estudios de Cultura Maya* III:149–67.

— 1964. "Historical data in the inscriptions of Yaxchilan, Part II," *Estudios de Cultura Maya* IV:177–201.

Pyburn, K. Anne 1998. "Smallholders in the Maya lowlands: Homage to a garden variety Ethnographer," *Human Ecology* 26:267–86.

Pyburn, K. Anne (ed.) 2004. *Ungendering Archaeology*, New York: Routledge.

Reents-Budet, Dorie 1994. *Painting the Maya Universe*, Durham, NC: Duke University Press.

Reilly, F. Kent 2002. "Female and male: The ideology of balance and renewal in elite costuming among the Classic Period Maya," in *Ancient Maya Gender Identity and Relations*, Lowell Gustafson and Amy Trevelyan (eds), pp. 319–28, Westport, CT: Greenwood Press.

Rice, Patricia C. 1981. "Prehistoric Venuses: Symbols of motherhood or womanhood?" *Journal of Anthropological Research* 37:402–14.

Richards, Colin, and Julian Thomas 1984. "Ritual activity and structured deposition in Later Neolithic Wessex," in *Neolithic Studies*, Richard Bradley and John Gardiner (eds), pp. 189–218, Oxford: British Archaeological Reports 133.

Ridgway, Brunilde 1987. "Ancient Greek women and art: The material evidence," *American Journal of Archaeology* 91 (3):399–409.

Robin, Cynthia 2001. "Kin and gender in Classic Maya Society: A case study from Yaxchilan, Mexico," in *New Directions in Anthropological Kinship*, Linda Stone (ed.), pp. 204–28, Boulder, CO: Rowman and Littlefield.

— 2002. "Outside of houses: The practices of everyday life at Chan Noohol, Belize," *Journal of Social Archaeology* 2:245–68.

— 2003. "New directions in Classic Maya

household archaeology," *Journal of Archaeological Research* 11:307–56.

—— 2006. "Gender, farming, and long-term change: Maya historical and archaeological perspectives," *Current Anthropology* 47 (3):409–34.

Roosevelt, Anna C. 1988. "Interpreting certain female images in prehistoric art," in *The Role of Gender in Precolumbian Art and Architecture*, Virginia Miller (ed.), pp. 1–34, Lanham, MD: University Press of America.

Rosaldo, Michelle Zimbalist, and Louise Lamphere (eds) 1974. *Woman, Culture and Society*, Stanford: Stanford University Press.

Roscoe, Will 1991. *The Zuni Man-Woman*, Albuquerque, NM: University of New Mexico Press.

—— 1998. *Changing Ones: Third and Fourth Genders in Native North America*, New York: St. Martin's Press.

Roughgarden, Joan 2004. *Evolution's Rainbow: Diversity, Gender, and Sexuality in Nature and People*, Berkeley: University of California Press.

Ruscheinsky, Lynn 1995. "The construction and reproduction of gender hierarchy," in *Debating Complexity: Proceedings of the 26th Annual Chacmool Conference*, Daniel A. Meyer, Peter C. Dawson, and Donald T. Hanna (eds), pp. 629–34, Calgary: Chacmool Archaeological Association.

Russell, Pam 1993. "The Palaeolithic mother goddess: Fact or fiction?" in *Women and Archaeology: A Feminist Critique*, Hilary duCros and Laurajane Smith (eds), pp. 93–97, Department of Prehistory, Research School of Pacific Studies, Occasional Papers in Prehistory, No. 23, Canberra: Australian National University.

Schiffer, Michael B. 1987. *Formation Processes of the Archaeological Record*, Albuquerque: University of New Mexico Press.

Schmidt, Robert A. 2000. "Shamans and northern cosmology: The direct historical approach to Mesolithic sexuality," in *Archaeologies of Sexuality*, Robert A. Schmidt and Barbara L. Voss (eds), pp. 220–35, London: Routledge.

Seifert, Donna J. 1991. "Within site of the White House: The archaeology of working women," *Historical Archaeology* 25 (4):82–108.

Seifert, Donna J., and Joseph Balicki 2005. "Mary Ann Hall's house," *Historical Archaeology* 39 (1):59–73.

Seifert, Donna J., Elizabeth Barthold O'Brien, and Joseph Balicki 2000. "Mary Ann Hall's first class house: The archaeology of a capitol brothel," in *Archaeologies of Sexuality*, Robert A. Schmidt and Barbara L. Voss (eds), pp. 117–28, London: Routledge.

Seler, Eduard 1923. "Die Ruinen von Chich'en Itzá in Yucatan," *Gesammelte Abhandlungen zur amerikanischen Sprach- und Alterthumskunde*, 5, pp. 197–388, Berlin: A. Asher.

Serra, Mari Carmen, and Yoko Sugiura 1987. "Funerary rites at two historical moments in Mesoamerica: Middle and Late Formative," in *Studies in the Neolithic and Urban Revolutions: The V. Gordon Childe Colloquium, Mexico, 1986*, Linda Manzanilla (ed.), pp. 345–51, BAR International Series 349, British Archaelological Reports, Oxford.

Sigal, Pete 2005. "The *Cuiloni*, the *Patlache*, and the abominable sin: Homosexualities in early colonial Nahua society," *Hispanic American Historical Review* 85: 555–94.

—— 2007. "Queer Nahuatls: Sahagun's faggots and sodomites, lesbians and hermaphrodites," *Ethnohistory* 54 (1):9–34.

Soffer, Olga 1997. "The mutability of Upper Palaeolithic art in Central and Eastern Europe: Patterning and significance," in *Beyond Art: Pleistocene Image and Symbol*, Margaret W. Conkey, Olga Soffer, Deborah Statmann, and Nina Jablonksi (eds), pp. 239–62, San Francisco: California Academy of Sciences and University of California Press.

— 2004. "Recovering perishable technologies through use wear on tools: Preliminary evidence for Upper Paleolithic weaving and net making," *Current Anthropology* 45:407–13.

Soffer, Olga, James Adovasio, and David C. Hyland 2000. "The 'Venus' figurines: Textiles, basketry, gender and status in the Upper Paleolithic," *Current Anthropology* 41:511–37.

Soffer, Olga, and Margaret W. Conkey 1997. "Studying ancient visual culture," in *Beyond Art: Pleistocene Image and Symbol*, Margaret Conkey, Olga Soffer, Deborah Starmann, and Nina Jablonksi (eds), pp. 1–16, San Francisco: California Academy of Sciences and University of California Press.

Soffer, Olga, Pam Vandiver, Bohuslav Klima, and Jiri Svoboda 1993. "The pyrotechnology of performance art: Moravian Venuses and Wolverines," in *Before Lascaux: The Complex Record of the Early Upper Paleolithic*, Heidi Knecht, Anne Pike-Tay, and Randall White (eds), pp. 259–76, Boca Raton, FL: CRC Press.

Sørensen, Mary Louise Stig 2000. *Gender Archaeology*, Cambridge: Polity Press.

Spector, Janet D. 1983. "Male/female task differentiation among the Hidatsa: Toward the development of an archaeological approach to the study of gender," in *The Hidden Half: Studies of Plains Indian Women*, Patricia Albers and Beatrice Medicine (eds), pp. 77–99, Washington, DC: University Press of America.

Spector, Janet D., and Mary K. Whelan 1989. "Incorporating gender into archaeology classes," in *Gender and Anthropology: Critical Reviews for Research and Teaching*, Sandra Morgen (ed), pp. 65–94, Washington, DC: American Anthropological Association.

Spencer-Wood, Suzanne 2006. "Feminist gender research in classical archaeology," in *Handbook of Gender in Archaeology*, Sarah Nelson (ed.), pp. 295–329, Lanham, MD: AltaMira.

Spude, Catherine H. 2005. "Brothels and saloons: An archaeology of gender in the American West," *Historical Archaeology* 39 (1):89–106.

Stahl, Ann B. 1993. "Concepts of time and approaches to analogical reasoning in historical perspective," *American Antiquity* 58:235–60.

Stone, Andrea 1988. "Sacrifice and Sexuality: Some Structural Relationships in Classic Maya Art," in *The Role of Gender in Precolumbian Art and Architecture*, Virginia Miller (ed.), pp. 75–103, Lanham, MD: University Press of America.

— 1991. "Aspects of impersonation in Classic Maya art," in *Sixth Palenque Round Table, 1986*, Virginia Fields (ed.), pp. 194–202, Norman: University of Oklahoma Press.

— 1995. *Images from the Underworld: Naj Tunich and the Tradition of Maya Cave Painting*, Austin: University of Texas Press.

Storey, Rebecca 1998. "Mothers and daughters of a patrilineal civilization: The health of females among the Late Classic Maya of Copán, Honduras," in *Sex and Gender in Paleopathological Perspective*, Anne L. Grauer and Patricia Stuart-Macadam (eds), pp. 133–48, Cambridge: Cambridge University Press.

Sweely, Tracy L. 1998. "Personal interactions: The implications of spatial arrangements for power relations at Ceren, El Salvador," *World Archaeology* 29:393–406.

— 1999. "Gender, space, people and power at Ceren, El Salvador," in *Manifesting Power: Gender and the Interpretation of Power in Archaeology*, Tracy Sweely (ed.), pp. 155–71, London: Routledge.

Tanner, Nancy, and Adrienne Zihlman 1976. "Women in evolution, Part I: Innovation and selection in human origins," *Signs* 1:585–608.

Taube, Karl 1985. "The Classic Maya maize god: A reappraisal," in *Fifth Palenque Round*

Table, 1983, Virginia Fields (ed.), pp. 171–81, San Francisco: Pre-Columbian Art Research Institute.

Taylor, Walter W. 1948. *A Study of Archeology*, Menasha, WI: American Anthropological Association.

Thompson, Philip C. 1982. "Dynastic marriage and succession at Tikal," *Estudios de Cultura Maya* 14:261–87.

Tolstoy, Paul 1989. "Coapexco and Tlatilco: Sites with Olmec materials in the Basin of Mexico," in *Regional Perspectives on the Olmec*, Robert J. Sharer and David C. Grove (eds), pp. 85–121, Cambridge: Cambridge University Press.

Tozzer, Alfred M. 1941. *Landa's Relación de las cosas de Yucatan*, translator and editor, Papers of the Peabody Museum, Vol. XVIII, Cambridge, MA: Peabody Museum of Archaeology and Ethnology, Harvard University.

Treherne, Paul 1995. "The warrior's beauty: The masculine body and self-identity in Bronze Age Europe," *Journal of European Archaeology* 3:105–44.

Trigger, Bruce 2006. *A History of Archaeological Thought*, second edition, Cambridge: Cambridge University Press.

Tringham, Ruth E., and Margaret W. Conkey 1998. "Rethinking figurines: A critical view from archaeology of Gimbutas, the 'Goddess,' and popular culture," in *Ancient Goddesses*, Lucy Goodison and Christine Morris (eds), pp. 22–45, London: British Museum Publications.

Trinkhaus, Erik, and Jiri Svoboda (eds) 2006. *Early Modern Human Evolution in Central Europe: The People of Dolní Vèstonice and Pavlov*, Oxford: Oxford University Press.

Vandiver, Pamela, Olga Soffer, Bohuslav Klima, and Jiri Svoboda 1989. "The origins of ceramic techology at Dolní Vèstonice, Czechoslovakia," *Science* 246:1002–1008.

— 1990. Venuses and wolverines: The origins of ceramic technology at Dolní Vèstonice ca. 26,000 BP," in *Ceramics and Civilization*, vol. 5, W. David Kingery (ed.), pp. 13–81, Westville, OH: American Ceramics Society.

Voss, Barbara L. 2000. "Colonial sex: Archaeology, structured space, and sexuality in Alta California's Spanish colonial missions," in *Archaeologies of Sexuality*, Robert A. Schmidt and Barbara L. Voss (eds), pp. 35–61, London: Routledge.

— 2006. "Sexuality in archaeology," in *Handbook of Gender in Archaeology*, Sarah Nelson (ed.), pp. 365–400, Lanham, MD: AltaMira Press.

Walde, Dale, and Noreen Willows (eds) 1991. *The Archaeology of Gender: Proceedings of the 22nd Annual Chacmool Conference*, Calgary: Department of Archaeology, Calgary University.

Walker, Susan 1983. "Women and housing in classical Greece: The archaeological evidence," in *Images of Women in Antiquity*, Averil Cameron and Amelie Kuhrt (eds), pp. 81–91, London: Croom Helm.

Webster, David, and Nancy Gonlin 1988. "Household remains of the humblest Maya," *Journal of Field Archaeology* 15:169–90.

Weedman, Kathryn 2006. "Gender and ethnoarchaeology," in *Handbook of Gender in Archaeology*, Sarah Nelson (ed.), pp. 247–94, Lanham, MD: AltaMira Press.

Weismantel, Mary 2004. "Moche sex pots: Reproduction and temporality in ancient South America, *American Anthropologist* 106 (3):495–505.

Weston, Kath 1993. "Lesbian/gay studies in the house of anthropology," *Annual Review of Anthropology* 22:339–67.

White, Christine D. 2005. "Gendered food behaviour among the Maya: Time, place, status and ritual," *Journal of Social Archaeology* 5 (3):356–82.

White, Christine D., Rebecca Storey, Fred J. Longstaffe, and Michael W. Spence 2004. "Immigration, assimilation, and status in the ancient city of Teotihuacan: Stable isotopic evidence from Tlajinga 22," *Latin American Antiquity* 15:176–98.

Whitehead, Harriet 1981. "The bow and the burden strap: A new look at institutionalized homosexuality in Native North America," in *Sexual Meanings: The Cultural Construction of Gender and Sexuality*, Sherry Ortner and Harriet Whitehead (eds), pp. 80–115, Cambridge: Cambridge University Press.

Wilk, Richard M., and Wendy Ashmore (eds) 1988. *Household and Community in the Mesoamerican Past*, Albuquerque: University of New Mexico Press.

Wilk, Richard M., and William L. Rathje (eds) 1982. *Archaeology of the Household: Building a Prehistory of Domestic Life*, special issue of *American Behavioral Scientist* 25.

Wilkie, Laurie A. 2003. *The Archaeology of Mothering: An African-American Midwife's Tale*, London: Routledge.

Wilkie, Laurie A., and Katherine Howlett Hayes 2006. "Engendered and Feminist Archaeologies of the Recent and Documented Pasts," *Journal of Archaeological Research* 14:243–64.

Wilkie, Laurie A., and George W. Shorter, Jr. 2001. *Lucretia's Well: An Archaeological Glimpse of an African-American Midwife's Household*, University of South Alabama Archaeological Monograph 11, Mobile, AL: University of South Alabama Center for Archaeological Studies.

Wylie, Alison 1985. "The reaction against analogy," *Advances in Archaeological Method and Theory* 8:63–111.

— 1988. "'Simple' analogy and the role of relevance assumptions: Implications of archaeological practice," *International Studies in the Philosophy of Science* 2:134–50.

— 1991. "Gender theory and the archaeological record: Why is there no archaeology of gender?" in *Engendering Archaeology*, Margaret W. Conkey and Joan Gero (eds), pp. 31–54, Oxford: Blackwell.

— 1992. "The interplay of evidential constraints and political interests: Recent archaeological research on gender," *American Antiquity* 57:15–35.

— 1996. "The constitution of archaeological evidence: Gender politics and science," in *The Disunity of Science*, Peter Galison and David J. Stump (eds), pp. 311–43, Palo Alto: Stanford University Press.

— 2002. *Thinking from Things: Essays in the Philosophy of Archaeology*, Berkeley: University of California Press.

Yamin, Rebecca 2005. "Wealthy, free, and female: Prostitution in nineteenth century New York," *Historical Archaeology* 39 (1):4–18.

Yanagisako, Sylvia, and Jane Fishburne Collier (eds) 1987. *Gender and Kinship: Essays Toward a Unified Analysis*, Stanford: Stanford University Press.

Yates, Tim 1993. "Frameworks for an archaeology of the body," in *Interpretive Archaeology*, Christopher Tilley (ed.), pp. 31–72, Providence, RI: Berg.

Zihlman, Adrienne 1978. "Women in evolution, Part II: Subsistence and social organization among early hominids," *Signs* 4:4–20.

— 1981. "Women as shapers of the human adaptation," in *Woman the Gatherer*, Frances Dahlberg (ed.), pp. 75–120, New Haven: Yale University Press.

Acknowledgments

This book would not have been written without the encouragement of my editor at Thames & Hudson, Ian Jacobs, who not only engaged me in a number of conversations about the potential for such a book, but also gave the original draft a sympathetic and yet critical read, leading me to work hard to improve it. At Thames & Hudson, senior editor Julia MacKenzie greatly improved the text and eliminated as much repetition and obscurity as she could; what remains obscure or repetitive is at least intentional on my part. Sally Nicholls was my ideal of an illustrations researcher, and to the extent that there is a visual element in this book, it owes a great deal to her tenacity with me and others. The people to whom I owe intellectual debts are all obvious from my citation of their work in the text. This book is unusual for me because I have not presented any part of it previously as public lectures or conference papers. But the main arguments and cases cited have formed the basis for a course I initiated in 2006 and continue to teach at the University of California, Berkeley, in the interdisciplinary Discovery Courses program in the College of Letters and Science. I am indebted to the former Dean of the Undergraduate Division of Letters and Science, Robert C. Holub, and Alix Schwartz, Director of Academic Planning of the Undergraduate Division, for encouraging me to develop L&S 180A, "Archaeologies of Sex and Gender." The more than 180 students who have so far passed through the course inspired me to try to clarify precisely why archaeology matters when it comes to understanding our contemporary world, and to them I owe almost the greatest debt. But as ever, the one person without whom this book would never have been completed is my husband, Rus Sheptak, who has heard every piece of the argument as a story unfolding during many walks and drives and who listens for what I am trying to say and helps me find the right words. It is totally fitting that the title of the book was his suggestion. I could not have done this without him.

Picture Credits

Index